A Poetry Teacher's Toolkit

Book 2: Rhymes, Rhythms and Rattles

Other titles in this series:

A Poetry Teacher's Toolkit Book 1: Words and Wordplay
A Poetry Teacher's Toolkit Book 3: Style, Shape and Structure
A Poetry Teacher's Toolkit Book 4: Language and Performance

A Poetry Teacher's Toolkit

Book 2:
Rhymes, Rhythms and Rattles

Collette Drifte and Mike Jubb

David Fulton Publishers
London

David Fulton Publishers Ltd
Ormond House, 26–27 Boswell Street, London WC1N 3JZ
www.fultonpublishers.co.uk

First published in Great Britain in 2002 by David Fulton Publishers

Note: The rights of Collette Drifte and Mike Jubb to be identified as the authors of this work have been asserted by them in accordance with the Copyright, Designs and Patents Act 1988.

British Library Cataloguing in Publication Data
A catalogue record for this book is available from the British Library.

ISBN 1-85346-819-3

Typeset by Kenneth Burnley, Wirral, Cheshire
Illustrations by Bethan Matthews
Printed and bound in Great Britain by Bell and Bain Ltd, Glasgow

Contents

For my Mum, because she loves poetry [C.D.]

For Tony Bradman, who took the time [M.J.]

The Authors

Collette Drifte is a former deputy head teacher who has 23 years' experience in both mainstream and special primary education. She has specialised in both learning difficulties and child language development and disorders, and spent nine years working as a special educational needs advisory teacher to mainstream practitioners. Now a freelance author, lecturer and in-service education and training (INSET) provider, her writing credits include: *Phonicability* (Hopscotch Educational Publishing 2000); *Including Lower-achievers in the Literacy Hour: Using Stories and Poems* (Hopscotch Educational Publishing 2001); *Foundations for the Literacy Hour* (Step Forward Publishing 2001); and *Special Needs in Early Years Settings* (David Fulton Publishers 2001). Other publications include articles in the *Times Educational Supplement* and *Practical Pre-School*, and regular articles and reviews for *Nursery World*.

Mike Jubb is a primary school teacher who lives in Hampshire with his two children, Nicky and Kevin. Having waited until middle age before discovering that he might be able to write, Mike has had many poems anthologised and his own collection, *Burblings of the Jubb-Jubb Bird*, is available for £4.50 (including post and packing) from Mike Jubb, PO Box 245, Fareham, Hants PO15 6YN.

Acknowledgements

We would like to thank the following, without whom these books would never have been written: Helen Fairlie, of David Fulton Publishers, for her untold patience in dealing with a never-ending stream of queries and for her valued suggestions; Alan Worth, also of David Fulton Publishers, for his efficient and professional friendliness in steering us through the production process; those friends and professionals who tried out the activities and made suggestions; staff and pupils of Rupert House School, Henley-on-Thames, Redlands Primary School, Fareham, Peel Common Junior School, Gosport and Crofton Hammond Junior School, Stubbington; and, finally, our families, for their support and tolerance, even when we were up the walls or in our rooms sulking.

Collette Drifte

Mike Jubb

The authors and the publishers would like to thank the following copyright holders for permission to include their work:

Paul Bright, for 'Yeti'.

Jane Clarke, for 'White Knuckle Ride' and 'Snow'.

Charlotte Druitt Cole, for 'The Clothes-Line', from *Poems for You, Book 3*, published by Collins, 1964, reprinted by permission of HarperCollins Publishers Ltd.

Berlie Doherty, for 'Grandpa', from *Another First Poetry Book*, edited by John Foster and published by Oxford University Press, 1987, reprinted by permission of David Higham Associates.

Faber and Faber Ltd, for 'The Heron', by Ted Hughes, from *The Iron Wolf*, published by Faber and Faber Ltd.

Liss Norton, for 'The Last Mermaid'.

Ian Souter, for 'The Green Water Giant', from *A Green Poetry Paintbox*, edited by John Foster and published by Oxford University Press, 1994.

The Estate of J. R. R. Tolkien, for 'The Man in the Moon Stayed Up Too Late', from *The Adventures of Tom Bombadil*, published by George Allen and Unwin, 1962, reprinted by permission of HarperCollins Publishers Ltd.

Emma Woodward, for 'Henry the Eighth Doesn't Visit Relate'.

Every effort has been made to trace copyright holders, but in some instances this has not been possible. The publishers would like to apologise for any errors or omissions in this list, and would be grateful to be advised of any corrections which should be made to future editions of this book.

Introduction

The package deal

Even though my teaching days are over – they are now a source of anecdotes and amusing stories to weave into my lectures – I am aware that there are still unplugged holes that cause teachers to question 'Why doesn't somebody invent an xxx to do that?' or state 'Someone ought to write a book which covers that'. We aim to 'cover that' with this series of books, 'that' being poetry and the teaching thereof.

In my pre-National Curriculum days I taught a literature syllabus, both prose and poetry, which covered most, if not all (and more!), of the objectives in the National Literacy Strategy – nothing new there really. I can still remember spending lunchtimes and evenings searching through poetry anthologies for suitable poems to illustrate a specific teaching point – nothing new in that either. In fact, from comments made to me on my rounds since hanging up my satchel, this is still quite a problem. The 'big poetry hunt' eats into what precious little time teachers have left in their 24 hours after preparation, marking, form-filling, etc. I recall one child's face registering utter surprise as he realised I had a home to go to – 'Don't you sleep here, then, Miss?' he asked. Sometimes it felt as if I did!

We all know that there is a healthy supply of poetry anthologies available (many based on themes), which are beautifully produced, superbly illustrated and packed with, in some cases, hundreds of poems – but how does a teacher zoom straight to those that illustrate specific points such as alliteration, wordplay, metaphors and similes? This is where we come in. *A Poetry Teacher's Toolkit* is aimed at Key Stage 2 teachers who need to teach poetry as part of the National Literacy Strategy whether by choice, design or default. It brings together a collection of poems that offers quick access to such specific points, inspirational ideas and more formalised lesson plans, together with supporting photocopiable differentiated activity sheets. The book provides a complete package that should help teachers to maximise their limited preparation and research time.

The myth exploders

There is another, equally important, reason why this series of books was written. Poetry is often perceived as a medium that is 'difficult', 'highbrow', 'hard to teach' or 'not cool'. However you may feel about poetry, it is now a prominent part of the National Literacy Strategy.

In this series, we aim to demystify poetry in a fun way that will inspire enthusiasm in both you and the kids you teach. We offer ideas and suggestions that will both stimulate and excite anyone who happens to be in your room while you are 'doing' poetry. Reading and writing poetry is fun as well as educational, and we make no apologies for putting this message across with gusto! Activities are suggested that not only extend and consolidate the teaching points made in the lessons but also simultaneously – and almost unconsciously – foster an enjoyment of poetry by everyone.

The Toolkit

We are very aware that you, as teachers, are hard-pressed for time as well as bound by the requirements of the National Curriculum. *A Poetry Teacher's Toolkit* provides lesson plans that follow the framework of the Literacy Hour and support specific objectives in the National Literacy Strategy. The lesson plans are based on poems from the collection and include photocopiable activity sheets that support each teaching point and which are differentiated, thereby reducing preparation time. Many a teacher has told us that they would have our arms out of the sockets if we proffered such a book! It would be arrogant of us to suggest that these lesson plans are The Answer, but they offer a framework that you can either use as it stands, or tweak and cherry-pick to suit your own or your school's requirements. Because some of you may not normally 'teach' poetry, we have scripted the lessons. Before you gasp in outrage this is purely for guidance – the lessons can and should be delivered in your own personal style.

Chapter and verse

Each chapter follows the same format, which you will quickly become familiar with as you use the ideas and lessons:

- A list of featured poems and poets relevant to the chapter's contents.
- Ideas and suggestions for the reading, writing and performance of poetry by both children and teachers.
- More formalised lesson plans in line with the structure and recommendations of the Literacy Hour including relevant National Literacy Strategy objectives for Years 3–6 (at text, sentence and word level), materials needed, preparation required and scripted sessions.
- Photocopiable activity sheets differentiated for lower, average and higher achievers. Each sheet presents the same activity at appropriate levels and is differentiated as follows:
     sheets a or aa for the lower achievers
     sheets b or bb for the average achievers
     sheets c or cc for the higher achievers.
- The featured poems reproduced for reference.

We have offered the material in such a way that will allow you to use it at whatever level you want, whether as an activity done outside the Literacy Hour or as an integral part of the hour itself, and to whatever degree you want, such as incorporating several more of the activities into one of the lessons or taking a lesson plan as the basis for deeper exploration of the teaching point. Virtually all of the Literacy Hour lesson plans have at least one group activity suggestion from the previous part of the chapter, but you don't have to stick rigidly to that. You know your kids and the areas that need to be reinforced or consolidated. Use the Toolkit to pick and mix but, above all, have fun!

Rhymes, Rhythms and Rattles and the National Literacy Strategy – comfortable bedfellows

Year 3

Term 1

To read aloud and recite poems; to distinguish between rhyming and non-rhyming poetry and comment on the impact of layout; to express their views about a . . . poem, identifying specific words and phrases to support their viewpoint; to generate ideas relevant to a topic by brainstorming, word association, etc.; to collect suitable words and phrases in order to write poems and short descriptions; design simple patterns with words, use repetitive phrases; to use awareness of grammar to decipher new or un-familiar words; to take account of the grammar and punctuation . . . when reading aloud; to use word banks and dictionaries; to infer the meaning of unknown words from the context; to understand the purpose and organisation of the thesaurus and to make use of it to find synonyms.

Term 2

To . . . prepare poems for performance, identifying appropriate expression, tone, volume and use of voices and other sounds; to rehearse and improve performance, taking note of punctuation and meaning; to write new or extended verses for perfor-mance based on models of 'performance' poetry read, e.g. rhythms, repetition; to experiment with deleting words in sentences to see which are essential to retain meaning and which are not; to use word banks and dictionaries; to infer the meaning of unknown words from the context; to continue the collection of new words from reading and . . . make use of them in reading and writing.

Term 3

To select, prepare, read aloud and recite by heart poetry that plays with language or entertains; to recognise rhyme, alliteration and other patterns of sound that create effects; to write poetry that uses sound to create effects [through] distinctive rhythms; to use word banks and dictionaries; to infer the meaning of unknown words from the context.

Year 4

Term 1

To find out more about popular . . . poets; to write poems based on personal or imagined experience, linked to poems read; to list brief phrases and words; to experiment by trimming or extending sentences; to reread own writing to check for grammatical sense and accuracy; to use phonic/spelling knowledge as a cue, together with graphic, grammatical and contextual knowledge, when reading unfamiliar texts; to use word banks and dictionaries.

Term 2

To understand the use of figurative language in poetry and prose; to compare poetic phrasing with narrative/descriptive examples; to locate the use of simile; to identify different patterns of rhyme and verse in poetry; to develop use of settings in own writing, making use of work on adjectives and figurative language to describe settings effectively; to write poetry based on the structure and/or style of poems read; to write own examples of descriptive, expressive language based on those read and link to work on adjectives and similes; to understand the significance of word order, e.g. sentences can be reordered to retain meaning; to use phonic/spelling knowledge as a cue, together with graphic, grammatical and contextual knowledge, when reading unfamiliar texts; to use word banks and dictionaries.

Term 3

To understand the following terms and identify them in poems: verse, chorus, couplet, stanza, rhyme, rhythm, alliteration; to clap out and count the syllables in each line of regular poetry; to describe how a poet does or does not use rhyme; to read further . . . poems by a favourite writer, making comparisons and identifying familiar features of the writer's work; to write poems, experimenting with different styles and structures, discuss if and why different forms are more suitable than others; to produce polished poetry through revision; to identify the common punctuation marks . . . and respond to them appropriately when reading; to use phonic/spelling knowledge as a cue, together with graphic, grammatical and contextual knowledge, when reading unfamiliar texts.

Year 5

Term 1

To read a number of poems by significant poets and identify what is distinctive about the style or content of their poems; to analyse and compare poetic style, use of forms and the themes of significant poets; to respond to shades of meaning; to explain and justify personal tastes; to consider the impact of full rhymes, half-rhymes, internal rhymes and other sound patterns; to investigate and collect different examples of wordplay, relating form to meaning; to write metaphors from original ideas or from similes; to understand the need for punctuation as an aid to the reader; to discuss, proofread and edit their own writing for clarity and correctness; to use independent spelling strategies; to use dictionaries.

Term 2

To compile a class anthology of favourite poems with commentaries which illuminate the choice; to understand the difference between literal and figurative language . . . through discussing the effects of imagery in poetry and prose; to use the structures of poems read to write extensions based on these, e.g. additional verses, or substituting own words and ideas; to review and edit writing to produce a final form, matched to the needs of an identified reader; to understand how writing can be adapted for different . . . purposes; to consolidate the conventions of standard English; to use dictionaries and IT spell checks; to distinguish between homophones; to explore onomatopoeia; to investigate metaphorical expressions and figures of speech from everyday life.

Term 3

To select poetry, justify their choices; to explore the challenge and appeal of older literature through listening to older literature being read aloud, reading accessible poems, stories and extracts and discussing differences in language used; to use performance poems as models to write and produce poetry in published form through revising, redrafting and presentation; to secure the basic conventions of standard English; to understand how writing can be adapted for different audiences; to use a range of dictionaries and understand their purposes.

Year 6

Term 1

To articulate personal responses to literature, identifying why and how a text affects the reader; to contribute constructively to shared discussion about literature, responding to and building on the views of others; to write own poems experimenting with active verbs and personification; to produce revised poems for reading aloud individually; to revise the conventions of standard English; to adapt texts for particular . . . purposes; to use dictionaries; to understand how words and expressions have changed over time.

Term 2

To recognise how poets manipulate words: for their quality of sound, e.g. rhythm, rhyme, assonance; for their connotations; for multiple layers of meaning, e.g. through figurative language, ambiguity; to analyse how messages, moods, feelings and attitudes are conveyed in poetry; to read and interpret poems in which meanings are implied or multi-layered; to discuss, interpret challenging poems with others; to increase familiarity with significant poets and writers of the past; to parody a literary text; to continue work on grammatical awareness and sentence construction and punctuation; to use dictionaries and IT spell checks.

Term 3

To discuss how linked poems relate to one another by themes, format and repetition; to describe and evaluate the style of an individual poet; to comment critically on the overall impact of a poem, showing how language and themes have been developed; to write a sequence of poems linked by theme or form; to continue work on grammatical awareness and sentence construction and punctuation; to experiment with language.

Right, on with the motley – or at least the sessions, whether you wear funny togs or not! The main thing to remember is that you should all be having fun during these sessions, so throw caution and dignity to the wind, get yourself to the level of the kids and enjoy yourselves.

A 'Must Read' Chapter!

Read this chapter if you read none of the others!

'I get a fine warm feeling when I'm doing well, but that pleasure is pretty much negated by the pain of getting started each day. Let's face it, writing is hell.' (William Styron)

That just about sums up the love/hate affair that many professional writers have with their craft. But they are volunteers, and deserve no sympathy whatsoever.

The ones we **should** feel sorry for are the press-ganged kids who are obliged to 'write a story' or 'write a poem', whether they feel inspired or not (usually not!). For many of them, it really **must** be hell, and it can be pretty hellish for the teacher trying to inspire them too!

This is a 'bullet-point' chapter, designed to help you all towards poetry heaven.

Your attitude

- If you're uncertain about teaching poetry, you're reading the right book.
- If you're not yet enthusiastic about poetry, FAKE IT for now because you soon will be! As in everything else, enthusiasm from the teacher equals enthusiasm from the kids.
- You won't overcome barriers in the mind of a child until you overcome any that **you** might have in yours.
- Nobody likes **all** poetry, so give yourself a chance and find out what you **do** like. Children's poetry is an easy read – soak yourself in it.
- Start a loose-leaf collection of your favourites, and make your own booklist. Leave it lying around for the kids to browse through and let them see you browsing through it.
- Please don't think of poetry as a 'subject' to be covered. If you want success, it should be ever-present.
- Algebra is for schooldays. Poetry is for life.
- Petition for an INSET day with an established children's poet.
- Arrange for a performance poet to come into school.
- It's good to ring the changes – try a different poet each term.

Creating a poetry atmosphere

- Have a good, and constantly changing, selection of poetry books and tapes in your classroom, and allow time for the children to explore them.
- Make your own poetry tapes, and encourage the children and tame parents to do the same.
- Read a new poem to your class each day, maybe in the ten minutes before lunch (see 'Appreciation and analysis' for a suggested strategy).
- Sometimes read narrative poetry at 'story time'.
- Get the children to write out, **at home**, the words of their favourite pop songs and adverts, and bring the transcripts in.
- Please don't just have a poetry 'unit' and think 'Well, I've done poetry now'. 'A little and often' will show that you really value poetry. You can slip a poem in almost anywhere by linking it with other themes, such as the weather or festivals. And if you can't find a poem to fit, write one yourself. Yes you can!
- Display a 'Poem of the Week'. Choose a reasonably short one so that each child can copy it into a special book, along with their own favourites, to create a personal anthology. This is copying with a purpose – it's allowed.
- Use poetry for handwriting practice.
- Use all your display skills to show off children's own poetry in exciting ways; 'publication' of their work is vital.
- Encourage and reward learning poetry by heart. It's fun.
- Encourage performance of poems learnt. The sense of achievement is huge.
- Would you, or one of your colleagues, be willing to start a school 'Poetry Choir'? (See *A Poetry Teacher's Toolkit* Book 4, Ch. 4.)
- Create illustrated class anthologies either by theme, or with each child choosing a favourite.
- **Every classroom should have a flipchart**. When you're writing a poem with the whole class, or brainstorming, or making word collections, or experimenting with any kind of wordplay, it's worth keeping the results as a possible future resource.
- TOP TIP for encouraging children to write poetry: write poetry yourself. Yes you **can**!

On being a writer

- Teachers often say that they can't write poetry – but they ask children to!
- Poetry has something special going for it. Not everyone can write a novel, but **everyone** can write poetry.
- If, for argument's sake, Shakespeare lives at the top of the poetry skyscraper, and nursery rhymes dwell on the ground floor, it follows that there is a room for everyone.
- Everyone **can** write poetry and every primary school teacher **should** write poetry.
- 'The worst thing you write is better than the best thing you didn't write' (Unknown).
- 'If you would be a writer, first be a reader' (Allan W. Eckert).
- Children learn to speak through imitation, not by constantly being corrected. Is there a lesson for writing here?

- 'Read everything . . . trash, classics, good and bad, and see how they do it. Read! You'll absorb it. Then write' (William Faulkner).
- Some people think that it's unreasonable to expect the whole class to write about the same thing at the same time. Well, many of the poems that **I** write come about because an anthologist has requested poems about a particular subject. This 'restriction' frees my mind of other topics and tells me what to concentrate on. If all the children are writing about the same thing, ideas start buzzing around. We don't want outright copying, but writers are always pinching (sorry, 'adapting') each other's ideas.
- 'Writing is a form of therapy; sometimes I wonder how all those who do not write, compose or paint can manage to escape the madness, melancholia, the panic fear which is inherent in a human situation' (Graham Greene).

Inspiration

Hopefully, you will find much in this series to inspire both you and your children, but here are a few quotations on the subject:

- 'I write when I'm inspired, and I see to it that I'm inspired at nine o'clock every morning' (Peter De Vries). In other words, you have to **make** it happen.
- 'The art of writing is the art of applying the seat of the pants to the seat of the chair' (Mary Heaton Vorse).
- 'The ideal view for daily writing, hour on hour, is the blank brick wall of a cold storage warehouse' (Edna Ferba).
- 'Imagination is more important than knowledge' (Einstein).

Drafting and redrafting

- 'The beautiful part of writing is that you don't have to get it right the first time, unlike, say, a brain surgeon' (Robert Cormier).
- 'It is perfectly okay to write garbage – as long as you edit brilliantly' (C. J. Cherryh).
- 'There is no great writing, only great rewriting' (Justice Brandeis).
- 'I have made this letter longer than usual, only because I have not had the time to make it shorter' (Blaise Pascal).
- 'In composing, as a general rule, run your pen through every other word you have written; you have no idea what vigour it will give to your style' (Sydney Smith).
- Successful creative writing is not about individual lessons, it's about creating an atmosphere in which children feel free to take risks. And if you weren't already convinced about the importance of rewriting, I hope you are now. Your mission, should you choose to accept it, is to persuade the children!
- Children should feel liberated by the thought that professional writers don't get it right first time; that they don't begin at the beginning, go through the middle, get to the end . . . and that's it.
- The beginning/middle/end thing is an important concept, for the reader or listener; but the **writer** doesn't have to work that way, providing the outcome has structure.

- We need to relax children about creative writing. We must persuade them that they can't get it 'wrong' in a first draft. Of course, we can help them to improve their writing but, if we're too judgemental, we'll scare them off.
- For the first draft: **no rubbers and no spellings**. They slow down creativity. The most important thing is to get words onto paper as quickly as possible. Errors can be put right and improvements made – later. It's counter-productive to ask children to be creative, and then burden them (or allow them to burden themselves) with secretarial matters that could be sorted out after the poem or story has evolved.
- 'Show, don't tell', e.g. 'She was angry' merely TELLS us about her anger; but 'She threw her hairbrush at the mirror' SHOWS us her anger. It's far more powerful writing. (See *A Poetry Teacher's Toolkit* Book 4, Ch. 1.)
- When writing, we tend to concentrate on the visual to the neglect of our other senses. That's a waste of resources. (Again, see *A Poetry Teacher's Toolkit* Book 4, Ch. 1.)
- Always be SPECIFIC. Don't say 'I saw a dog', say 'I saw a white poodle'. There are many opportunities to improve writing by this simple trick of the trade. (For more information about being specific, see *A Poetry Teacher's Toolkit* Book 4.)
- The second draft is not just a neater copy of the first.
- All words are not born equal. If you can cut out a word, and the poem doesn't 'miss' it, then cut it out (the same applies to prose).
- The poem's title is always the last thing that I write so that it fits what I have written and not the other way round.
- 'Don't be afraid to be bad. Every drop of high-performance gasoline starts as crude oil' (R. E. Lee).

Grammar

- Grammar to a poet is almost a total irrelevance.
- By 1870, there were no professors of modern English at Oxford and Cambridge.
- Grammar is based on Latin and ancient Greek . . . wonderful languages for grammarians because they are DEAD, and the rules can be fossilised. That's why we have such weary commandments as: never begin a sentence with 'And' or 'But'; never split an infinitive; never end a sentence with prepositions such as 'with', 'on', 'to', 'for'.
- 'In the beginning, God created the heaven and the earth. And the earth was without form and void; and darkness was on the face of the deep. And the spirit of God moved upon the face of the waters. And God said, "Let there be light": and there was light. And God called the light day, and the darkness he called night. And the evening and the morning were the first day.' Five sentences beginning with 'And'.

Grammar has its place, but it shouldn't get in the way of what we want to say, or the way we want to say it.

Ne'er more these things a poet does

- A modern poet strives not to be 'poetical', 'e'en' for the sake of rhythm or rhyme.
- We don't change the usual order of words.
- We don't use 'poetical' contractions such as: ne'er, e'en, 'tis, 'twas, o'er, 'twixt, 'neath.
- We don't put in a 'do' or 'did' where it wouldn't be used in normal speech. So, 'I cried' is fine, but 'I did cry' is OUT.
- 'Cut out all those exclamation marks. An exclamation mark is like laughing at your own joke' (F. Scott Fitzgerald).
- We don't use 'poetical' exclamations such as: O!, Oh! and Ah!
- We avoid words that don't occur in normal conversation. So: woe, befall, adieu, thee, thine, fain, etc. are all OUT.
- We avoid clichés and overworked phrases.
- We would rather write unrhymed poetry, or prose, than settle for second or third best words just to achieve a rhyme. The aim is that every word should be exactly the right one.
- We never pop in an extra word, or two, just to make the rhythm right. Every word in a poem must 'earn its keep'.
- Like a clown on a trapeze, knowing the rules, we might occasionally break them. This is also known as Mike Jubb's 'get-out' clause!

(Thanks to Colin Archer for these ideas.)

Appreciation and analysis

- Reading poetry out loud is the best way of appreciating its musical qualities and making it come alive.
- When you read a poem to children, think PERFORMANCE. Practise beforehand, making sure that you can read it with proper pace, timing and inflection.
- Putting on different voices may not come naturally to you but, if a poem calls for it, at least try a different pitch. After all, you do that when you're singing.
- Children often rush when reading aloud; **you** should err on the side of slowness, 'savour the flavour'. (See *A Poetry Teacher's Toolkit* Book 4, Ch. 4.)
- If you can perform poetry well, no child will ever leave your class not liking poetry . . . despite what some children may **say**.
- In a 10- or 15-minute session, read the poem once, and then ask the children to listen for something specific, such as an example of alliteration or a metaphor, during a second reading. Finish with a third reading.
- If you take up the 'Poem of the Week' idea, try to read it aloud several times during the week, highlighting a different aspect each time.
- The words 'analysis' and 'appreciation' sound boring, and may have connotations with indifferent poetry teaching during your own schooldays. These are requirements of the National Literacy Strategy, but they don't **have** to be boring. Well taught, they are not.
- Poetry for children should firstly be for pleasure, and recognising the tricks of the

writer's trade can add to that pleasure. But, in a short session it's better to select just one technique than to dissect the poem totally.

The Internet

You will find quite a few references to the Internet throughout this book and the other volumes in the series. If you haven't discovered surfing the World Wide Web with a purpose yet, there is a vast amount of free information, ideas and lesson plans out there just waiting for you.

1 I Got Rhythm

Featured poems

The Man in the Moon Stayed Up Too Late by J. R. R. Tolkien
From a Railway Carriage by R. L. Stevenson
Extracts from *The Song of Hiawatha* by H. W. Longfellow
The Pancake by Christina Rossetti
Cool Cat by Mike Jubb
White Knuckle Ride by Jane Clarke
The Last Mermaid by Liss Norton
Daffodils by William Wordsworth

'Poetry is to prose as dancing is to walking.' (John Wain)

Rhythm is basic – it's programmed into us. As individuals, we were enveloped by the rhythms within our mother's body (her heartbeat was iambic, as a matter of interest). And we are still surrounded by rhythm, and its cousin . . . pattern.

We Got Rhythm

Rhythm in your breathing, rhythm in your heartbeat,
Rhythm in your clapping and the tapping of your feet;
Rhythm when you swim, rhythm when you run;
Rhythm in the rising and the setting of the Sun;
Rhythm in the rain, and the chattering of teeth,
Rhythm in a caterpillar measuring a leaf;
Rhythm in a clock, and a telephone ringing;
Rhythm in a waterfall, and songbirds singing;
Rhythm in the wavelets lapping on a beach,
Rhythm in writing, rhythm in speech.

A rhythm may be noisy, or it may not make a sound,
Like the Rhythm of the Stars as they slowly dance around.   M.J.

This chapter aims to build on the rhythm work started in *A Poetry Teacher's Toolkit* Book 1, 'Words and Wordplay': in the 'Syllables' section of Chapter 2 and in the 'Onomatopoeia' section of Chapter 3.

'Rhythm' isn't synonymous with 'meter', of course. Meter is rhythm with rules; it establishes a pattern. But poetry was **spoken** yonks before any rules were written down. So I don't think we need to bother Key Stage 2 children with meter in the technical sense: iambs and youambs and pentathingies (especially as I'm not too hot on that stuff myself!). Anyway, it would stifle youngsters, which hopefully is why the National Literacy Strategy doesn't even mention the word 'meter'.

John Clare's *Pleasant Sounds* (p. 103) is a good example of a non-rhyming poem that revels in the natural rhythm of words, but has no formal meter. However, if kids absorb a 'feel' for meter along the way (which of course they do) then all well and good. Absorption is the best way of learning. The more they hear and perform poetry, the more the children will absorb. The more they absorb, the better writers they will be (see *A Poetry Teacher's Toolkit* Book 4, Ch. 4).

Here is an example of a 'found' poem:

Education, Education, Education

It looks as if my 'old' school has fallen
into the Blunkett Pit.
The new Head has,
as I expected,
removed all hope
of a humanitarian, joyous
creative, loving
caring, reflective
experimental, peaceful environment,
in favour of
a point-scoring, rigid,
false, regimented . . . ,
Oh how I could go on.

I got out in time,
and so have half the staff,

but the children can't.

Those words were written to me by a friend, before the 2001 General Election, as part of an e-mail. All I have done is to set them out so that they **look** like a poem, and I've added the title. When I first read the passage, it 'called' to me to be a poem. And I believe that it does work as a poem, partly because it came from the heart, but also because ordinary everyday English has a natural rhythm.

It's this natural rhythm, and not meter or rhyme, that is the essence of all English poetry (see *A Poetry Teacher's Toolkit* Book 3, Ch. 2 for more information about 'found' poetry and 'free' verse).

But, of course, meter and rhyme **do** join forces to create the sound patterns in many thousands of poems.

J. R. R. Tolkien was a master of rhythm and rhyme. This is the start of a poem called *Errantry* from his collection *The Adventures of Tom Bombadil* (see Further Reading):

> There was a merry passenger,
> a messenger, a mariner:
> he built a gilded gondola
> to wander in, and had in her
> a load of yellow oranges
> and porridge for his provender;
> he perfumed her with marjoram
> and cardamon and lavender.

To me, that is exquisite. Without any full rhymes, it contains so much that I'm trying to encourage throughout this series, and to achieve as a writer myself. Apart from its perfectly flowing rhythm, it has near-rhymes, half-rhymes, assonance, alliteration, enjambment (a line running into the next, see below) and a mid-line caesura (the pause after 'wander in', see below).

But listing the separate devices doesn't tell the half of it, does it? Notice how the word 'gilded' has both assonance, echoing the earlier 'built', and alliteration with 'gondola'. This is craftsmanship of the highest order. We haven't reproduced the whole of this poem in our anthology, but we have included Tolkien's *The Man in the Moon Stayed Up Too Late* (p. 35).

Before I talk about that poem, however, I want to mention two important terms: enjambment and caesura. If you're not familiar with the words, please don't be put off by the sound of them – they're dead easy, and they can make all the difference to the writing, the appreciation, and the performance of poetry.

Enjambment and caesura

Enjambment is the continuation of a sentence, without pause, beyond the end of a line; in the fragment from *Errantry* above, for example, 'he built a gilded gondola / to wander in'. Caesura means a pause or break; it is often highlighted by punctuation, but it can also be a natural pause . . . which is frequently the case in haiku, for instance.

A poem that has caesura only at the **end** of lines, and at the end of **all** of its lines (i.e. with no enjambment) lacks an element of fluidity. If it also has a strict meter and rhyming pattern, it encourages a 'sing-songy rumty-tumty' reading, with insufficient notice being taken of the meaning. Enjambment and caesura can be an important part of the difference between poetry and doggerel.

Consider *Daffodils* by William Wordsworth (p. 46). I make no apology for its inclusion **yet again**. It's through no fault of its own that it has become a cliché poem to some people. Those people will quite cheerfully quote 'I wandered lonely as a cloud', putting a full stop in their voice after 'cloud'. But this is what is written:

> I wandered lonely as a cloud / that floats on high o'er vales and hills

If anything, there should be a slight pause after 'wandered'. And again:

> Continuous as the stars that shine
>   And twinkle on the Milky Way,
> They stretch'd in never-ending line
>   Along the margin of a bay

There is no caesura after 'shine'; therefore the first two lines should be read:

> Continuous as the stars that shine/and twinkle on the Milky Way

If the reader **does** pause after 'shine' (and later after 'line'), the emphasis is then put on the rhyme, and not on the meaning. I think there is a **very** slight natural pause after 'line'; certainly not enough to stop the flow.

In this way, meter and rhyme are allowed to **blend** into the piece, almost camouflaged; they are part of the poem's musicality, but are not the main feature, the centre of attention.

Lastly:

> The waves beside them danced, but they
>   Outdid the sparkling waves in glee;
> A poet could not but be gay
>   In such a jocund company;
> I gazed, and gazed, but little thought
> What wealth the show to me had brought

There is a mid-line caesura after 'danced', so the first two lines should be read:

> The waves beside them danced,
> but they/outdid the sparkling waves in glee

This ensures that the rhyming of 'they' with 'gay' is kept in the background, where it belongs; the same applies to 'thought' and 'brought'. Rhyme can take care of itself; we don't need it thrust down our gullets.

Great poems like *Daffodils* are not written, they are composed. (For more about the performance of poetry, see *A Poetry Teacher's Toolkit* Book 4.)

The Man in the Moon Stayed Up Too Late by J. R. R. Tolkien (p. 35)

The subject of this poem demonstrates one of my favourite maxims with children: 'Ideas for poems are everywhere'. Tolkien takes the *Hey diddle diddle* nursery rhyme and embellishes it; enriches it with detail, character, and with fun in his mastery of the language.

The first five stanzas largely set the scene and introduce the characters, adding the Man in the Moon, plus the landlord and ostler of an inn, to those from the original rhyme.

On first hearing this poem, at what stage will the children begin to twig what it's about? Having given them all the clues, Tolkien unfolds the story with a jaunty rhythm (technically, iambic feet in a 4–3–4–4–3 line pattern) with an ABBA rhyming scheme.

Apart from using many of the tricks of the trade, which are explored throughout this volume (alliteration, assonance, internal rhyme, personification, anthropomorphism, simile), there are other points of writing interest in the poem.

- In the first stanza, the poet chooses to describe the hill as 'grey'. Quite a contrast with the 'merry old inn'.
- In stanza two, Tolkien has the fiddle 'purring low', reflecting the fact that the cat is playing it.
- Stanzas one to five inclusive are written in the present tense, suggesting that the inn and all the characters are still out there somewhere.
- Being round, the Man in the Moon '**rolled** beneath his chair'; and they 'rolled' him up the hill.
- In stanza eight, 'the Sun'll be rising' shows how two syllables can effectively be made into one, which can be important for a 'tight' meter.
- In a couple of places, 'The **white hor**ses of the Moon' and 'They **rolled** the Man **slow**ly **up** the hill', Tolkien deviates from his strict iambic rhythm.
- Tolkien uses exclamation marks, the archaic 'hornéd', and the 'poetical' exclamation 'O!' which are all best avoided in modern poetry – unless you're good! (See *A Poetry Teacher's Toolkit* Book 3, Ch. 1.)

Syllables

So, moving on from the exploration of the natural rhythm in names (*A Poetry Teacher's Toolkit* Book 1), you could open up this area of interest with contrasts, such as that between short, sharp words like 'bridge' and 'charging', and more flowing words like 'kingfisher' and 'whispering'.

Illustrate the point with Stevenson's *From a Railway Carriage* (p. 38), in which the impression of speed is created by using mostly one-syllable and two-syllable words.

WRITING ACTIVITY: From a railway carriage

Before asking children to compose a new verse for a poem, you could devise exercises like the following for them, where they simply have to come up with their own appropriate words.

Faster than (scooters), faster than witches,
Trees and (   ), (   ) and ditches;
And (ing) along like a bull at a gate,
(   ):
All the sights of the country and town
(   );
It's not like the pictures I see in a book,
(   ).

Obviously, we're looking for rhymes here as well. And, hopefully, I've made that comparatively easy. Chapter 2 of this volume deals more fully with rhyme, but this would be a good time to emphasise that a rhyme must be appropriate. In this instance, 'wait', 'late' and 'fete' could all be made to fit, whereas 'Kate', 'bait' and 'hate' are perhaps less likely, and would probably lead to a weaker result if 'forced' into the poem.

Some children might try adapting the second verse of Stevenson's poem. The more able could write a third of their own.

Compare the 'speed' of *From a Railway Carriage* with *Slumbering Lullaby* below.

WRITING ACTIVITY: Fluttering thunderstorm

With the children, collect nouns that have the same rhythm pattern as '**butt**erfly' (I looked it up, and it's called a 'dactyl') such as '**tel**ephone' and '**mic**roscope', and write them separately on small cards; the more the better. Similarly, with adjectives of the same pattern, such as '**whis**pering' and '**floun**dering'. Keeping the two word banks separate, the children can do 'lucky dips' to link words together randomly, giving results like 'chattering butterfly' and 'arguing roundabout'.

Get the children to use one of their phrases to kick off a poem. Tell them that they don't **have** to keep to that rhythm, or to rhyme their poem, but there's a model below if you think it's appropriate.

Random is creative. It's new ground. Who knows what may be discovered, and where the writing journey will lead, if we give children the courage to follow.

Slumbering Lullaby

Slumbering lullaby butterfly dream
Silvery summery watery day
Magical musical kingfisher stream
Whispering secrets and flying away   M.J.

I don't know what it means – and I wrote it! But it has atmosphere. The natural qualities of the chosen words give the piece a slow, lazy, impressionistic feel. It's a poem that came not from the mind, the heart or the soul, but from the ear. It wasn't written for a specific purpose, but when I decided to call it 'A Spell for Sleeping', it found a publisher!

The next two writing activities demonstrate the way I often set about writing a poem: I collect together a load of words and phrases that might be suitable, and then I try to fit some of them together. It's like building a dry-stone wall, or doing a jigsaw puzzle. If two words work well together for me, I keep them in; if not, I try something else and keep building until I have created the best poem I can.

WRITING ACTIVITY: Fish and chips

As a weekend or half-term 'homework' (for your own class or even the whole year group), get the children to try to involve their parents in collecting phrases that fit the 'Fish and Chips' pattern. There are scores, probably hundreds, of them:

Mum and Dad, Up and Down, Chalk and Cheese, Warts and All; even a phrase with more syllables, like 'Thunder and Lightning', can be collected because it still contains only two that are stressed, poor things. And don't forget rhyming slang: Apples and Pears, Dog and Bone (see *A Poetry Teacher's Toolkit* Book 1, Ch. 2 and Ch. 3).

Promise the kids a team point, or whatever, for every one they come up with **that isn't on anybody else's list**. Eventually, the complete collection should be displayed on large pieces of card. Challenge your colleagues to come up with any that you have overlooked. This is a phrase bank worth keeping.

I reckon that's a worthwhile exercise on its own, but if you want a writing challenge: construct poems that use **only** phrases from your list, even if they're just four lines long. It doesn't **have** to rhyme, but one way of starting would be to pick out pairs of phrases that do rhyme, such as 'to and fro', 'come and go'. So you might write:

Back and forth
To and fro
Here and there
Come and go

This is treating writing as a problem-solving activity, which is what it **always** is really. And with a large enough phrase bank, it could be an ongoing activity. The poems are in there, just waiting to be discovered.

> Chalk and cheese, Husband and wife
> On and off, Trouble and strife
> This and that, Rights and wrongs
> Over and over, Hammer and tongs (or 'tongues'!)
> More and more, Rant and rail
> Worse and worse, Tooth and nail
> Bitter and twisted, Scream and shout
> Thunder and lightning, Over and out
> Again and again, On and on
> Love and marriage, Dead and gone   M.J.

Well, I'm in that kind of mood today – tomorrow I'll write something more positive. Your 'Fish and Chips' phrase bank will be useful again for the next writing activity.

 ## WRITING ACTIVITY: Make a march

If you took up the idea from *A Poetry Teacher's Toolkit*, Book 1, Chapter 2 of using place names to devise a marching poem, you could build on this experience by asking the children to write a poem about marching to a band using 'ordinary' words.

Get them marching in the hall or playground first, both to command: 'Left, right, left, right' or 'Hup, two, three, four. Hup, two, three, four'; and to music in 2/4 time (*76 Trombones* would fit in well with the poem I'm about to write). You could also show that sequence of marching elephants in Disney's *Jungle Book*.

With the children, brainstorm two-syllable words, where the stress is on the first syllable (look up 'trochee', if you're interested). Words such as 'marching' and 'soldiers' come readily to mind, but others such as 'sometimes' and 'only' might come in handy. Nothing will be wasted, because even if you don't use a certain word in *this* poem, you can build up a (trochaic) word bank.

In addition to these words, get the children to use a thesaurus to find suitable words within relevant areas of meaning. Looking up 'march' in my *Roget's Thesaurus*, I selected 'motion, gait, 245n'. This entry suggested words such as: movement, tempo, forward, backward, progress, bustle, rapid, restless, rhythm, after, current, traffic, transport, travel, treading, tramping, stamping, stepping, pacing, striding, strutting. There are others, but that'll do for now.

Then I go through the same exercise with 'soldier 722n', ignoring anything violent, to see if that gives me any ideas: army, private, corporal, sergeant, major, captain, colonel, general, column. Maybe.

Now for some 'sound' words. I am not going to list them all here, but the point I'm making is that I'm in no hurry to start constructing this poem until I have assembled a good selection of building bricks.

It's not easy to write a poem containing **only** two-syllable words, of course. So you might feel you need to do some oral work on how combinations of words can have the same rhythmic effect. This is where your 'Fish and Chips' phrase bank could be useful again. For example:

Up and **down**, they're **always mar**ching

Here's a first verse to get you all going. It could even be used as a refrain.

Soldiers **mar**ching **round** the **show**ground,
Keeping **tempo** **with** the **band**;
Hup two three four, **rest**less **rhyth**m,
Every soldier **spick** and **span**.   M.J.

Four points of interest:

1. There is a 'rest' after both 'band' and 'span'. It's comparable to a rest in music. You could fill the one after 'band' with 'It's', for example.
2. A stress is deliberately missed out on the word 'three'.
3. 'band' and 'span' is not a perfect rhyme – it's a near-rhyme, and it's certainly near enough for me (see Ch. 2).
4. Lastly, you can point out to the children that there are some words 'missing'. In prose, the last line, for instance, would read: 'Every soldier **is** spick and span'. It's not necessary in poetry because, in poetry, only important words survive the rewriting process (see p. 8 for more about drafting).

Jane Clarke's *White Knuckle Ride* (p. 44) illustrates three of these points:

• There's a 'rest' at the end of a number of lines, e.g. after 'escape' and 'cry':

No escape, (I)
Want to cry. (I'm)
At the top now

You may say, 'So what?', but it does give you flexibility when you're juggling with syllables, with emphasis and with meaning to achieve a tight rhythm.

- In the fourth stanza, 'numb/fun' is a near-rhyme.
- In prose terms, there are many words missing, e.g. 'My heart's thumping, and my stomach's churning'. It needs to be pointed out regularly to children that, in poetry, we don't have to write in 'proper' sentences. As a rule of thumb, the more you can prune out, and still retain your meaning, the better. (See *A Poetry Teacher's Toolkit* Book 3, Ch. 1.)

THE LITERACY HOUR: YEARS 3 AND 4

National Literacy Strategy objectives: Years 3 and 4

Year 3
- To write poetry that uses sound to create effects [through] distinctive rhythms.
- To take account of the grammar and punctuation . . . when reading aloud.
- To continue the collection of new words from reading . . . and make use of them in reading and writing.

Year 4
- To clap out and count the syllables in each line of regular poetry.
- To understand the significance of word order, e.g. sentences can be reordered to retain meaning.
- To use phonic/spelling knowledge as a cue, together with graphic, grammatical and contextual knowledge, when reading unfamiliar texts.

Chosen poem

Extracts from *The Song of Hiawatha* by H. W. Longfellow (p. 39)

Materials needed

Copies of the chosen poem (see 'Preparation')
Percussion instruments
Marker pens
Copies of different four-line sections of the poem for Group 1.
Dictionaries and thesauruses
Pens, pencils, writing paper/books
Activity sheets (see 'Preparation')
'Rhythm' cards (see 'Preparation')

Preparation

Make an enlarged copy of the poem.

Make copies of the activity sheets for each child, according to achievement level (photocopiable sheets 1a, 1b, 1c on pp. 28–30).

Make two sets of 'rhythm' cards, one of nouns and one of adjectives with the same rhythm as 'butterfly' (see above, p. 17). For example, 'butterfly', 'elephant', 'roundabout', 'violin', 'telephone', 'leprechaun', 'skeleton', 'microscope', 'maniac', frying-pan', 'telescope' and 'caramel'; 'excellent', 'feverish', 'delicate', 'wonderful', 'arguing', 'slippery', 'flavoursome', 'marvellous', 'favourite' and 'narrower'. Also prepare a few blanks for the group's own words.

With the whole class

- Show the title of the poem to the children and ask them what they think it means. Can they suggest who Hiawatha might be? Explain that he was a legendary chief of the native-American Onondaga tribe. Do they know of other native-Americans (real or fictional)? For example, Pocahontas or Sitting Bull (of the Battle of Little Bighorn, 1876). Tell them that the poem was written by Longfellow in 1855. Today they'll be exploring two extracts from *The Song of Hiawatha*. (Do they know what an extract is?)

- Share the poem with the children, reading it carefully to enable them to get the flavour of the descriptions and atmosphere. Spend a bit of time looking at some of the lines that have an 'old-fashioned' word order, such as 'Learned of every bird its language' or 'Froze the ice on lake or river'. Did this word order prevent the children from understanding the meaning? Can they suggest why or why not?

- Ask the children to tell you what they imagine when reading the poem. For example, the birds and animals in the forest sharing their secrets with Hiawatha, or the frozen countryside caught in the solid grip of winter. Encourage them to choose lines that support what they are saying.

- Ask the children what 'syllables' are. If necessary, remind them and spend a few moments discussing and clapping the syllables in some of their names.

- Tell the children you are going to read part of the poem again and they should try to count the number of syllables in each line. Read several lines slowly enough to enable them to hear the number of syllables. Can they tell you how many there are in each line? (Eight) Clap a rhythm of eight beats and encourage the children to join in. Once they have the rhythm, read some more of the lines from the poem, making sure you speak one syllable per clap. When you have finished, ask the children what this rhythm might represent, e.g. the drums of a native-American ceremony.

- Ask a volunteer to choose any line and, as a class, discuss the emphasis or stress on each word or pair of words in it. Let other children choose different lines until they realise that each line is composed of pairs of one-syllable words, or single two-syllable words, with a stress or emphasis on the first syllable. (Except for 'Hiawatha', which has four syllables, although still with the emphasis on the first and third, and 'covering' which has three but is spoken as two.) For example,

> **Learned** of / **every** / **bird** its / **lang**uage
> **How** the / **beavers** / **built** their / **lodg**es
> **Through** the **forest**, **round** the **vill**age
> **In** the / **ghast**ly, / **gleam**ing / **for**est

- Once this rhythm has been worked out, start clapping it together until all the children have joined in. Then read part of the poem again, making sure you keep with the children's rhythm. Can the children suggest what this rhythm could represent? Tell them there is no right or wrong answer – it is all open to interpretation, as long as they can give a reason for their reply.

• Ask some of the children to use the percussion instruments to beat the rhythm of the poem and encourage the others to join in with you to read it once again. Remind the instrument players that the first beat is stronger than the second. Have fun putting voices and instruments together! (Perhaps not a good idea to do this bit on a day when you have a migraine . . .)

Group and independent work (differentiated groups)

Group 1

Give the children the copies of the four-line sections of the poem. Ask them to decide which syllables in each line are stressed and circle them with a coloured marker pen. According to achievement level, this activity could be done singly, in pairs or as a group.

Group 2

Work with the children to practise beating the rhythm of the poem, using the percussion instruments. (This may have to be done away from the main classroom.)

Group 3

Give out copies of sheets 1a (for lower achievers), 1b (for average achievers) and 1c (for higher achievers). Make sure the children can see a copy of the chosen poem.

Group 4

Give the children the dictionaries and thesauruses and ask them to find other two-syllable words that have a stress on the first syllable. They should list the words they find. Explain that their words don't have to be connected to the poem.

Group 5

Place the 'rhythm' cards face down on the table in their separate piles. Let the children play 'Lucky Dip', taking one card from each pile to make a random link, such as 'slippery telephone' or 'favourite skeleton' (see activity above, p. 17). Challenge them to find more words with the same rhythm and write them on the blank cards.

Plenary session (whole class)

• Have a 'Record Requests' session – invite the children to ask you to read any section of the extract they like, up to four lines each. Spend a few minutes reading their 'requests', encouraging them to join in.
• Using the instruments, played by different children from those in the whole-class session, recite the whole extract once again.
• Did the children enjoy exploring this poem? Can they tell you why or why not?

THE LITERACY HOUR: YEARS 5 AND 6

National Literacy Strategy objectives: Years 5 and 6

Year 5
- To analyse poetic style . . . and justify personal tastes.
- To understand the need for punctuation as an aid to the reader.
- To distinguish between homophones.

Year 6
- To contribute constructively to shared discussion about literature, responding to and building on the views of others.
- To revise the conventions of standard English.
- To experiment with language.

Chosen poem

Cool Cat by Mike Jubb (p. 42)

Materials needed

Copies of the chosen poem (see 'Preparation')
Activity sheets (see 'Preparation')
Photocopiable sheet A (see 'Preparation')
Percussion instruments
Cassette recorder/player
Blank cassette
Copies of the poem for Group 4 (two copies per child plus some for 'mistakes')
Scissors
Thesauruses

Preparation

Enlarge the poem or make a copy for each child.

Make copies of the activity sheets for each child, according to achievement level (photocopiable sheets 1aa, 1bb, 1cc on pp. 31–33).

Make enough copies of the poem for Group 4.

Make copies of photocopiable sheet A (p. 34) for Group 5.

With the whole class

- Talk about the title of *Cool Cat*: what do the children think it means? Do we use that phrase in relation to humans? Why do they think we use it when speaking of cats? Do they know of any 'cool' cats? For example, Felix in the television adverts or Macavity from *Old Possum's Book of Practical Cats* by T. S. Eliot.
- Share the poem with the children, letting them see the text as you read. Try to read it in a way that brings out the jauntiness of the rhythm. When you have finished reading ask the children whether they like the poem. Encourage them to say why or why not.
- Spend some time talking about the poem. What does 'nine' in the first line mean? Why does the Cool Cat say he has 'eight' at the end of the poem? Why has the poet used ' ! X ! X ! X ! X ! ' ? (To imply the near-miss between the car and the Cool Cat.) What does 'in my prime' mean? What words or phrases has the poet used to show that the Cool Cat is independent and a freewheeler? ('I'm gonna love ya and leave ya', 'I'm on my own', 'I like to be alone', 'I'm just a . . . Rollin' stone'.) How does he show that the Cool Cat has a high opinion of himself? ('I'm a Casanova Cat', 'all the little lady cats/Are looking for a treat', 'it's your lucky day I'm gonna pass your way', 'I'm lookin' good'.)
- Can anybody tell you the rhyme pattern that runs through almost all of the poem? (Groups of four lines, with a pattern of AABA.) Focus on the phrases 'I'm feline fine', 'Meeow my' and 'I'm feline great'. Why are these good examples of wordplay? Do the children know what 'feline' means? If not, ask a volunteer to check in a dictionary. How are 'feline' and 'Meeow my' (half) homophones? ('Feelin' and 'Me-oh-my'.) How are they also a play on words? How does the poet move from the refrains 'to be with you' and 'play with me' back into the body of the poem? Point out that he uses the final word of the refrain as a starter for the next line. ('**You** got grace' and '**Mee**ow my'.)
- Tell the children you're going to read the poem again and when they think they can hear its rhythm, they should join in. Begin your reading, accompanying yourself by clicking your fingers or clapping your hands in the rhythm of the poem. Encourage the children to join in as you read and keep time. When you have finished, ask the children what the rhythm of the poem makes them think of. For example, rap or 'ordinary' pop songs, etc. Ask for volunteers to play some of the percussion instruments and have one more class recital, accompanied by the players.

(NB: When the children are confident about identifying rhythm in poetry encourage them to pay heed to it as an integral part of their performances. See *A Poetry Teacher's Toolkit* Book 4.)

Group and independent work (differentiated groups)

Group 1

Have some fun with the percussion instruments, and practise beating out the rhythm of the poem at the same time as reciting it. Choose the length to practise according to achievement level. (This may need to be done away from the main classroom.)

Group 2

Give the children copies of activity sheets 1aa (for lower achievers), 1bb (for average achievers) and 1cc (for higher achievers) to complete. Make sure the group has access to thesauruses.

Group 3

Give the children the cassette recorder/player and the blank cassette. Help them to choose a section of *Cool Cat* and then ask them to practise reciting it together. Let them record their work and tell them to replay and re-record until they are happy that they have captured the rhythm and jauntiness of the poem in their performance.

Group 4

Give out copies of the poem and the scissors. Ask the children to discuss and agree how the poem could be cut into sections. They should then cut up their copies and experiment with the order of the sections to make another poem. When they have agreed an order, they should recite it to see whether the rhythm and the meaning have changed. Encourage them to try several versions before agreeing the final one.

Group 5

Give out photocopiable sheet A and challenge the children to collect phrases that fit the 'Fish and Chips' rhythm pattern (see activity above, p. 18). According to achievement level, this could be done individually, in pairs or as a group.

Plenary session (whole class)

- Ask the group that recorded their recital to play the cassette to the rest of the class. Did they find it easy to do this activity? Can they say why or why not? Is there anything they would do differently if they were set the activity again?
- Ask someone from the group that cut up the poem to read their new poem to the rest of the class. Did they find this activity easy? Why or why not?
- Did the class as a whole enjoy exploring this poem? Why or why not? Encourage the children to express an opinion about the poem, saying why they have their view.

SHEET 1a

Name _____

Read the extracts from *The Song of Hiawatha* explored in the whole-class session.

Look at these words and put a coloured circle around the stressed syllable. One has been done for you.

secrets   summer   beavers   rabbit   brothers

Now look at these lines from *The Song of Hiawatha* and put a coloured circle around the stressed syllables in each line. There's an example to help you.

Oh the **long** and **dre**ary **Win**ter!
Oh the **cold** and **cru**el **Win**ter!

Ever thicker, thicker, thicker
Froze the ice on lake and river,

Write some more words from the poem which have a stress on the first syllable:

_____   _____   _____   _____

SHEET 1b

Name _____

Read the extracts from *The Song of Hiawatha* explored in the whole-class session.

Look at these words and put a coloured circle around the stressed syllable. One has been done for you.

beavers   secrets   rabbit   brothers

winter   thicker   forest   summer

Now look at these lines from *The Song of Hiawatha* and put a coloured circle around the stressed syllables in each line. There's an example to help you.

Oh the **long** and **dre**ary **Win**ter!
Oh the **cold** and **cru**el **Win**ter!

Ever deeper, deeper, deeper
Fell the snow o'er all the landscape,
Fell the covering snow and drifted
Through the forest, round the village.

Write some more words from the poem which have a stress on the first syllable:

_____   _____   _____

_____   _____   _____

SHEET 1c

Name _____

Read the extracts from *The Song of Hiawatha* explored in the whole-class session.

Look at these words and put a coloured circle around the stressed syllable. One has been done for you.

secrets   beavers   weakness   thicker

village   brothers   forest   summer

wigwam   footprints   winter   rabbit

Now look at these lines from *The Song of Hiawatha* and put a coloured circle around the stressed syllables in each line. There's an example to help you.

Oh the **long** and **dre**ary **Win**ter!

Oh the **cold** and **cru**el **Win**ter!

Hardly from his buried wigwam

Could the hunter force a passage;

With his mittens and his snow-shoes

Vainly walked he through the forest,

Sought for bird or beast and found none,

Saw no track of deer or rabbit

Write some more words from the poem which have a stress on the first syllable:

_____   _____   _____   _____

_____   _____   _____   _____

SHEET 1aa

Name _____

Read these lines from *Cool Cat* by Mike Jubb:

    I'm strolling down the street

    In my white slipper feet

    Yeh, all the little lady cats

    Are looking for a treat

What is the rhyme pattern? _____   _____   _____   _____

Put some words in the blank spaces to make a new verse for *Cool Cat*. It doesn't have to rhyme. You could use a thesaurus or dictionary to help you.

    I'm _____ down the street

    In my white _____ feet

    Yeh, all the _____ lady cats

    Are looking for a treat

Write some more words to do with cats:

_____   _____   _____

_____   _____   _____

SHEET 1bb

Name _____

Read these lines from *Cool Cat* by Mike Jubb:

But it's your lucky day

I'm gonna pass your way

I can spare a little lovin'

If you wanna stop and play

What is the rhyme pattern? _____   _____   _____   _____

Put some words in the blank spaces to make a new verse for *Cool Cat*.
It doesn't have to rhyme.

But it's your _____ day

I'm gonna _____ your way

I can _____ a little lovin'

If you wanna stop and _____

Write some more words to do with cats:

_____   _____   _____   _____

_____   _____   _____   _____

SHEET 1cc

Name _____

Read these lines from *Cool Cat* by Mike Jubb:

    You got grace

    You got a lickable face

    I'm gonna love ya and leave ya

    And you'll never find a trace

What is the rhyme pattern? _____   _____   _____   _____

Put some words in the blank spaces to make a new verse for *Cool Cat*.
It doesn't have to rhyme.

    You got _____

    You got a _____ face

    I'm gonna _____ and _____

    And you'll never _____

Write some more words to do with cats:

_____ _____ _____ _____ _____

_____ _____ _____ _____ _____

PHOTOCOPIABLE SHEET A

Name _____

Read these 'Fish and Chips' phrases:

Mum and Dad	Up and Down	Chalk and Cheese
Left and Right	Cat and Mouse	Laugh and Cry

Now find or make up some 'Fish and Chips' phrases yourself:

_____   _____
_____   _____
_____   _____
_____   _____
_____   _____
_____   _____
_____   _____
_____   _____
_____   _____
_____   _____
_____   _____

The Man in the Moon Stayed Up Too Late

J. R. R. Tolkien

There is an inn, a merry old inn
    beneath an old, grey hill,
And there they brew a beer so brown
That the Man in the Moon himself came down
    one night to drink his fill.

The ostler has a tipsy cat
    that plays a five-stringed fiddle;
And up and down he runs his bow,
Now squeaking high, now purring low,
    now sawing in the middle.

The landlord keeps a little dog
    that is mighty fond of jokes;
When there's good cheer among the guests,
He cocks an ear at all the jests
    and laughs until he chokes.

They also keep a hornéd cow
    as proud as any queen;
But music turns her head like ale,
And makes her wave her tufted tail
    and dance upon the green.

And O! the row of silver dishes
    and the store of silver spoons!
For Sunday there's a special pair,
And these they polish up with care
    on Saturday afternoons.

The Man in the Moon Stayed Up Too Late (continued)

The Man in the Moon was drinking deep,
    and the cat began to wail;
A dish and a spoon on the table danced,
The cow in the garden madly pranced,
    and the little dog chased his tail.

The Man in the Moon took another mug,
    and then rolled beneath his chair;
And there he dozed and dreamed of ale,
Till in the sky the stars were pale,
    and dawn was in the air.

The ostler said to his tipsy cat:
    'The white horses of the Moon,
They neigh and champ their silver bits;
But their master's been and drowned his wits,
    and the Sun'll be rising soon!'

So the cat on his fiddle played hey-diddle-diddle,
    a jig that would wake the dead:
He squeaked and sawed and quickened the tune,
While the landlord shook the Man in the Moon:
    'It's after three!' he said.

They rolled the Man slowly up the hill
    and bundled him into the Moon,
While his horses galloped up in rear,
And the cow came capering like a deer,
    and a dish ran up with a spoon.

The Man in the Moon Stayed Up Too Late (continued)

Now quicker the fiddle went deedle-dum-diddle;
    the dog began to roar,
The cow and the horses stood on their heads;
The guests all bounded from their beds
    and danced upon the floor.

With a ping and a pong the fiddle-strings broke!
    the cow jumped over the Moon,
And the little dog laughed to see such fun,
And the Saturday dish went off at a run
    with the silver Sunday spoon.

The round Moon rolled behind the hill,
    as the Sun raised up her head.
She hardly believed her fiery eyes;
For though it was day, to her surprise
    they all went back to bed!

From a Railway Carriage

R. L. Stevenson

Faster than fairies, faster than witches,
Bridges and houses, hedges and ditches;
And charging along like troops in a battle,
All through the meadows the horses and cattle:
All of the sights of the hill and the plain
Fly as thick as driving rain;
And ever again, in the wink of an eye,
Painted stations whistle by.

Here is a child who clambers and scrambles,
All by himself and gathering brambles;
Here is a tramp who stands and gazes;
And there is the green for stringing the daisies!
Here is a cart run away in the road
Lumping along with man and load;
And here is a mill and there is a river:
Each a glimpse and gone for ever!

Extracts from *The Song of Hiawatha*

H. W. Longfellow

Then the little Hiawatha
Learned of every bird its language,
Learned their names and all their secrets,
How they built their nests in Summer,
Where they hid themselves in Winter,
Talked with them whene'er he met them,
Called them 'Hiawatha's Chickens'.
Of all beasts he learned the language,
Learned their names and all their secrets,
How the beavers built their lodges,
Where the squirrels hid their acorns,
How the reindeer ran so swiftly,
Why the rabbit was so timid,
Talked with them whene'er he met them,
Called them 'Hiawatha's Brothers'.

*   *   *

Oh the long and dreary Winter!
Oh the cold and cruel Winter!
Ever thicker, thicker, thicker
Froze the ice on lake and river,
Ever deeper, deeper, deeper
Fell the snow o'er all the landscape,
Fell the covering snow, and drifted
Through the forest, round the village.
Hardly from his buried wigwam
Could the hunter force a passage;

The Song of Hiawatha **(continued)**

With his mittens and his snow-shoes
Vainly walked he through the forest,
Sought for bird or beast and found none,
Saw no track of deer or rabbit,
In the snow beheld no footprints,
In the ghastly, gleaming forest
Fell, and could not rise from weakness,
Perished there from cold and hunger.

The Pancake

Christina Rossetti

Mix a pancake,
Stir a pancake,
Pop it in the pan.
Fry the pancake,
Toss the pancake,
Catch it if you can.

Cool Cat

Mike Jubb

Well I'm a cat with nine
And I'm in my prime
I'm a Casanova Cat
And I'm feline fine
I'm strolling down the street
In my white slipper feet
Yeh, all the little lady cats
Are looking for a treat
Because I got style
I got a naughty smile
I'm gonna cross this street
In just a little while
    to be with you
    to be with you
    to be with you
    to be with
You got grace
You got a lickable face
I'm gonna love ya and leave ya
And you'll never find a trace
Because I'm on my own
I like to be alone
I'm just a swingin', strollin',
Rollin' stone
But it's your lucky day
I'm gonna pass your way
I can spare a little lovin'
If you wanna stop and

Cool Cat (continued)

play with me
play with me
play with me
play with
Meeow my
I got a twinkling eye
I'm gonna cross this street
So don't you be too shy
But what's this I see
Comin' straight at me
It's a crazy car driver
Tryin' to make me flee
So I look up slow
Just to let the man know
That I don't go any faster
Than I really wanna go.

! X ! X ! X ! X ! X ! X ! X !

Well I'm a cat with eight
I guess he couldn't wait
But I'm lookin' good and I'm feline great!

White Knuckle Ride

Jane Clarke

Heart thumping,
stomach churning.
Let me off!
Wheels keep turning.

No escape,
want to cry.
At the top now.
Going to die.

Lurch then p
          l
          u
          m
          m
          e
          t
screaming, shrieking,
knuckles white and
bladder leaking.

Spinning, swooping,
sick inside.
Screech to a halt,
terrified.

Stagger off,
stunned and numb.
Let's do it again!
It was fun!

The Last Mermaid

Liss Norton

Once we tumbled, laughing, through the waves,
Hand in hand and tail entwined with tail;
Sat chattering on rocks and combed our hair
And polished, with our friends, each glittering scale.

Once we raced huge breakers to the beach,
Rode plump and giggling dolphins round the bay;
We slept in sea-bed dormitories at night,
And sang sweet songs in mermaid choirs by day.

Then humans came; they filled our sea with filth
And foaming froth; with choking oil slicks,
With chemicals and radio-active waste –
And one by one my mermaid friends fell sick.

So now I swim and tumble by myself,
Searching for a friend to share my sea.
I sing sad solos, comb my hair alone;
There's just one mermaid left now – lonely me.

Daffodils

William Wordsworth

I wandered lonely as a cloud
    That floats on high o'er vales and hills,
When all at once I saw a crowd,
    A host, of golden daffodils,
Beside the lake, beneath the trees,
Fluttering, dancing in the breeze.

Continuous as the stars that shine
    And twinkle on the Milky Way,
They stretch'd in never-ending line
    Along the margin of a bay:
Ten thousand saw I at a glance,
Tossing their heads in a sprightly dance.

The waves beside them danced, but they
    Outdid the sparkling waves in glee;
A poet could not but be gay
    In such a jocund company;
I gazed, and gazed, but little thought
What wealth the show to me had brought:

For oft, when on my couch I lie,
    In vacant or in pensive mood,
They flash upon that inward eye
    Which is the bliss of solitude;
And then my heart with pleasure fills,
And dances with the daffodils.

2 Is Rhyme a Misdemeanour?

Featured poems

Snow by Jane Clarke
Monday Morning by John C. Head
Roses are Red, Anon.
John Bun, Anon.
Five Little Owls, Anon.
Yeti by Paul Bright
Bare Back Riding by Mike Jubb
Rockets by Mike Jubb
Henry the Eighth Doesn't Visit Relate by Emma Woodward
Changing My Little Brother's Nappy by Lisa Rhodes

'I'd rather be a great bad poet than a bad good poet.' (Ogden Nash)

Lavender's blue, Dilly Dilly,
Lavender's green;
If a poem doesn't rhyme, Dilly Dilly,
Some people believe
It's better than one that does.   M.J.

or

I sent my Love some roses,
I sent my Love some pinks;
I sent her a rhymeless poem,
And she told me that it's not a proper poem at all.   M.J.

It's a bit 'old hat' nowadays to pose the question: 'is rhyme a crime?' It may seem that way with **some** modern poetry, but rhyme has never gone out of fashion with children, nor with most adults.

All rhyming is contrived. The skill is in making it feel **un**-contrived; making the reader or listener believe that the particular word belongs there, and no other would do.

Snow by Jane Clarke (p. 73)

This is a gem of a poem that uses rhythm and some clever rhyming to capture, very concisely, the 'three ages of snow': when it's falling and fresh, when it's there to be played with, and when it becomes mucky.

Jane draws attention to the different stages of snow by choosing to rhyme the adjectives and descriptive phrases: White/bright/night/light, Deep/heaped/leap/sweep, Cold/old/hold. Those words also carry a stress, while the inspired line, 'Silent in the night snow', adds the connotation of Christmas by echoing the well-known carol.

The fact that there is no rhyme for 'sweep' in the last line of the second stanza doesn't matter a hoot, because the assonance of 'feet' and the internal rhyme of 'aglow snow' more than compensate. The same applies to 'go, snow' at the end of the third stanza.

The calligram:

Crystal petal snowflakes
>   s
>   e
>   t   t
>   l
>   e

is a nice touch that will add to children's appreciation of what is 'allowed' in today's poetry.

Of course, there is now a great deal of emphasis on rhyme within the National Literacy Strategy. And, if anything, I think there's a danger of highlighting it too much in primary schools. It is very useful in the teaching of reading, of course, but it's **much** harder for children to write a **good** or meaningful poem in rhyme than it is to write a worthwhile unrhymed poem.

Rhyme is an unnatural way of speaking. We don't go around speaking in rhyme . . . well, not all the time. And because it often goes hand in hand with a 'tight' meter, it clearly takes a great deal more effort, experience and sheer craftsmanship to get even a satisfactory result consistently. We all know the kind of rubbish children can come up with when the urge to rhyme takes control of the writing. Having said all that, rhyming is something that children **are** keen to do. And **of course** we should foster that keenness, as long as we ensure that they write poetry in a whole variety of styles, in the same way that we would want them to have a varied reading 'diet'. But when there are 'rules' (which is what rhyme and meter are), there is also the possibility of 'failure', which writing free verse doesn't have (see *A Poetry Teacher's Toolkit* Book 3, Ch. 2).

So, to minimise frustration (and poor writing) while they are learning the craft, I believe that children should be led gently into writing rhyming verse, so that meaning isn't left behind. If they dive in at the deep end, the results will often be unsatisfactory and unsatisfying.

There are several writing activities that include rhyme in Chapter 1 of this volume, and also in Book 1 of this set ('Words and Wordplay'). Here's another undemanding way in.

WRITING ACTIVITY: Rhyming couplets

This idea, for writing simple rhyming couplets, is a variation of the 'Fish and Chips' activity in Chapter 1, and can also be ongoing. Perhaps the children could have a section of their English book set aside for keeping their growing collection of couplets together. This could be a resource for inspiring longer poems as they gain experience and confidence.

Any phrase from the 'Fish and Chips' phrase bank may be chosen and used as the first line of a couplet. The child then has to come up with a second line that 'sounds right', giving consideration to rhyme, meter (hopefully absorbed) and, to a certain extent, meaning.

Now and again	Share and share	Mum and Dad	Far and away
You're a pain	You must be fair	Getting mad	Out for the day

Maybe some couplets could be combined to make a kind of sense.

Mum and Dad
Getting mad
Now and again
You're a pain

Except that 'You're' doesn't quite belong. So this would be a good time to remind the children that 'nothing is written in stone'.

Mum and Dad
Are getting mad;
Now and again
They're such a pain.

Again, to write a second and improved draft, we're free to abandon the parameters that we set ourselves at the beginning. So these lines:

Far and away
Out for the day
Mum and Dad
Getting mad

might redirect the poet's thoughts, and be redrafted to:

When we're out for the day,
Far and away,
Why does my Dad
Always get mad?

More able children now have another target: to write the second verse. Why **does** he get mad? (For more about 'drafting' see p. 8.)

WRITING ACTIVITY: Changing the rhyming structure

A trickier variation is to change the rhyming scheme, say from couplets to ABAB. So a possible first version:

Give and take
Cut the cake;
Share and share
You must be fair.

might be redrafted to:

You cut the cake
But you must be fair;
We've got to give and take
We've got to share and share.

or ABBA:

You've got to give and take,
You've got to share and share;
You've got to be fair,
So **I'll** cut the cake.

Assonance vs Near-rhymes vs Half-rhymes

I am a bit confused about some of this stuff myself, so I am giving some examples to clarify my own mind!

- 'Mean/street' is assonance. The words share the same vowel sound, but their final consonants are very different. This topic is considered in Chapter 3.
- 'Mean/dream' is near-rhyme because . . . you would get away with it. The final consonants are near enough in sound – a sort of assonance-plus.
- Multi-syllabic words in which the final syllable rhymes are half-rhymes: 'polish/relish' is one of the examples of a half-rhyme given in the glossary of the National Literacy Strategy. The other example given (pun/man) is a near-rhyme in my view. In many circumstances, if the poet is not a slave to full rhyme, these would be perfectly acceptable.

WRITING ACTIVITY: Near-rhyming couplets

Yet another variation of the previous writing activity reverts to couplets. This is the same set-up as before, except this time children are **forbidden** to use exact rhymes, and must compose their couplets using near-rhymes instead. (The definition being, remember, 'what you can get away with'.)

> Off and on/Things go wrong
> Scream and shout/Much too loud
> Thick and thin/Her and him
> Good and bad/In the lab [bit weak, that one]
> Hit and miss/catching fish

Writers, and readers, have to make up their own minds as to what works. As an exercise, this is harder than coming up with an exact rhyme because assonance is more difficult for children to spot. But it's good experience, and the knowledge that this technique is possible, and acceptable, will stand them in good stead. It gives them more options when they're stuck, and will hopefully free them from total slavery to full rhyme.

As before, the children can experiment with combining couplets, and also changing the rhyme pattern.

Half-rhymes

Half-rhymes rely on common endings: -ish (Cornish/Danish); -ive (active/permissive); -tion (nation/motion); -time (daytime/meantime); -ful (beautiful/awful). There must be thousands of them, and your *Penguin Rhyming Dictionary* will help you identify more (see below and p. 143).

 ## WRITING ACTIVITY: Introducing half-rhymes

You could do this one with the whole class first, before letting the kids have a go. Choose an ending such as '-less', and get suggestions for words that end with it. You might get some full rhymes (careless/hairless, harmless/charmless), but for this exercise you want a selection that are not:

   careless/heartless/timeless/soundless/worthless/thoughtless/harmless/sightless.

Explain to the children that these are half-rhymes, and they have to make up some 'half-rhyming' couplets, e.g.:

   My Mummy says I'm careless
   But Daddy says I'm harmless

Present the children with a few words that simply end in '-ess': press, tenderness, address. Do they think that these are half-rhymes too? Well, they are. So now the children can suggest a few more for your list, and try to come up with new couplets, or even quatrains, e.g.:

   You invited me to your party,
   but you're ever so slightly thoughtless;
   I **wanted** to come to your party,
   but you didn't write down the address.

The Rhyming Dictionary

At this point, I think I should confirm the existence of the rhyming dictionary, in case you didn't know about it. There's more than one on the market, but I would recommend *The Penguin Rhyming Dictionary*.

   To use it, all you do is look up the word you want to rhyme with, in the alphabetical section at the back. That will give you a reference number, which you turn to in the main body of the book, where you are presented with all the rhymes for that word, set out in groups of one syllable, two syllables, etc. In the case of a word like 'choose', you will also be referred to the 'oo' sound (as in 'blue'), because of the possibility of plurals, such as 'shoes'.

The Penguin Rhyming Dictionary and *Roget's Thesaurus* are the tools of my trade when I'm writing in rhyme. I use them in tandem because if I can't find a satisfactory rhyme for the word I want to use, I have to find an alternative for that word and start the process again, until I'm satisfied that I have matched up rhyme and meaning to the best of my ability. The same applies if my chosen word can't be fitted into my chosen meter.

WRITING ACTIVITY: Rhymes, rhythm and meaning

Here's a scenario: the children have to imagine that they have been taken to see a litter of puppies, with a view to choosing one. They have to write a rhyming couplet about it. One of the lines (it doesn't matter which) must be: '(But) Which one shall I choose?', e.g.:

> It's giving me the blues
> Which one shall I choose?

Restrict the time allowed to a couple of minutes. Tell the children that you would obviously prefer it to fit in with the scenario, but they MUST write something.

Once they've done that, get them to repeat the exercise but using an alternative to 'choose'. You can brainstorm the alternatives, or they can use a thesaurus; then they must come up with a new rhyming, or near-rhyming, line. This could be done four or five times. So they might have: 'I can't decide which one to choose/pick/have/select/take', each one part of a different couplet, e.g.:

> I've got to choose one quick
> But which one shall I pick?

> For goodness sake
> Which one shall I take?

Eventually, each child has to decide which is their best option, again giving consideration to rhyme, meter and meaning. This is the constant striving that is necessary when trying to write **good** rhyming poetry. In this way, we hope to avoid results like:

> I can't decide which one to choose,
> Because my dad is always out with his mates somewhere on the booze.

Invent your own scenarios, and repeat this exercise as often as you like/can. It's a path to the craft. But more about 'internal rhyme' later.

WRITING ACTIVITY: A riot of rhyme

This one takes things to the other extreme. The children collect as many words with the same rhyme as they can. They can brainstorm this in their groups, or use a rhyming dictionary. The writing task is to construct a nonsense poem using only the chosen rhyme.

Here are some likely rhymes to get you started: 'ease', 'newt', 'choose', 'bear', 'hat', 'nose', 'pet'. Working on their own, or in pairs, children will create different poems from the same collection of words.

Poems Don't Have to Rhyme

Way up in the trees
In the high Pyrenees
Some young chimpanzees
Were sitting at ease
With the birds and the bees
On their favourite trapeze
Eating their teas
Of peaches and peas
In the cool summer breeze
When their mother said, 'Please
Don't do a striptease
Or sneeze on the cheese
It encourages fleas
To squeeze your knees
Then you'll catch a disease
With a cough and a wheeze
Like the mumps or the meas(les)'

'Oh she's just a big tease'
said the apes and mon-keys

And now I sees
(With great expertise)
That's enough about these
Make-believe chimpanzees;

And I'm sure you agrees!   M.J.

It would be very boring to read a whole collection of poems like that. But, as a fun exercise, it's OK once in a while.

A word about 'nonsense' poems. When I visit schools, I'm at pains to tell children that 'nonsense' doesn't equal 'rubbish'. A nonsense poem can still (**must**) be well written and well crafted. In fact, it's a shame to use the word 'nonsense' really, because a good nonsense poem makes perfect sense **within its own world**, just as talking mice and flying snowmen make perfect sense in cartoons. (See *A Poetry Teacher's Toolkit* Book 4, Ch. 3.)

 WRITING ACTIVITY: Bout rhymes

I picked this one up surfing the web; apparently it used to be a popular parlour game. Somebody comes up with a number of rhyming pairs, and everyone else uses them (in any order) to write a poem. As long as all the words are used, the poem can be as sensible or silly as you like.

Try these pairs to write four couplets, or two quatrains.

food/mood; red/head; chase/face; crime/time

You could set this up as a game between pairs, or small groups of children . . . each giving the other a set of rhymes to try.

Internal rhyme

A great example of the power of this device is in the Beatles' song, *Penny Lane*:

He likes to keep his fire engine clean.
It's a clean machine.

In some ways, this topic belongs in the following chapter, 'Sounds Good', because the effect of internal rhyme is more closely related to the effect of assonance. But I'm going to deal with it here, because I feel like it. However, like assonance, it's a device to be used in moderation usually.

My poem, *Rockets* (p. 78), makes a big feature of internal rhymes in what would otherwise be free verse, e.g. dart/start, sky/high/fly, zip/rip.

WRITING ACTIVITY: Introducing internal rhyme

This is a fun variation of the 'One kick at a time' writing activity (see *A Poetry Teacher's Toolkit* Book 1, Ch. 1). It's better if the children don't have the word 'poetry' in mind while they are doing it, because we don't want meter to be a consideration this time.

The idea is that the children have to write just one sentence, but it must include a word that you give them, and it must also include a rhyme for the given word. So, you might give them the word 'snow', and they could write:

'I saw a crow in the snow' or 'I know it will snow on Christmas Day.'

There are various ways you could organise this activity. You could talk the children through each sentence (as in 'One kick at a time'), allowing them one minute for each sentence. Or, having talked them through one, you might write a list of 'kick-off' words on the board and let the children work through them. This has the advantage of freeing you, but the disadvantage of being less productive for some children!

These sentences can simply be a fun collection with no other purpose. Or each one could be the first line of a piece of free verse.

I saw a crow in the snow;
it bounced along
in black and white,

like an old movie.   M.J.

(See *A Poetry Teacher's Toolkit* Book 3, Ch. 2.)

You could even, with a little care, plan a sequence of 'kick-off' words. Tell the children that each sentence must follow on from the last, and the whole thing might just hang together. Try this one yourself, NOW!

'snow', 'out', 'fun', 'wet', 'day'

We're not necessarily going to call the result a poem, but it could turn into one with redrafting (for more about 'drafting' see p. 8). The main purpose of this activity is to acquaint the children with the existence of internal rhyme, which you can reinforce by reading them some examples from published poems.

Five Little Owls, Anon. (p. 75)

I have only just discovered this poem myself, and I think it's a great little performance piece, both for teachers and children. As I see it, these five owlets (as opposed to the species Little Owl) are in a row on a branch, waiting for Mum and Dad to return with food.

Fluffy/puffy and blinking/winking are not only internal rhymes but they 'suit' young owls perfectly; those words should receive extra emphasis. Without being either simile or metaphor, the double use of 'big round' is clearly comparing the owls' eyes to the full moon; these too need to be accentuated in performance. 'Tu-whit, Tu-whoo' is both alliterative and onomatopoeic, and I would perform the onomatopoeic 'Hoo hoo, Hoo hoo' with a giggle in my voice.

'Eyes/sky' is a near-rhyme. The writer 'gets away with it' because it doesn't jar on the ear in performance. In fact, most people wouldn't even notice that it wasn't a full rhyme.

Monday Morning by John C. Head (p. 74)

I suppose if the poet had put only one word per line:

Moaning
Groaning
Mumbling
Grumbling etc

you would have to say they were rhyming couplets. As it is, you could claim there's a lot of internal rhyme in this poem. Who cares? It's writing that counts, not definitions.

This poem emphasises the value of choosing the right title. By establishing that it's Monday morning at the outset, all the single-word phrases that follow immediately fall into place. This is a great poem for 'reading between the lines'. Take the sequence 'groping, soaping, howling': I read that as groping for the soap, and then getting suds in the eyes. Well-written poetry can convey a whole sentence in a single word.

Why 'splashing' **after** 'towelling'? I'm guessing that it's referring to splashing on some kind of 'smelly'. Ask the children: 'dashing' where?, 'buttering' what?, 'tying' what?, 'brushing' what?, 'cramming' what?, 'slamming' what? Does this sound like a leisurely preparation for school? Why not? ('Dashing', 'rushing', 'cramming', and maybe 'slamming', are all 'hurry-up type' words.) What else? (Short, sharp phrases always give the impression of urgency or speed or panic.)

 ## WRITING ACTIVITY: Chucking ducking

With the whole class, attempt to write a poem in the style of *Monday Morning*: *School, A Day at the Beach, Camping, Picnic, In the Snow, In the Woods, Haunted House*. Collect pairs of rhyming words together first, before you work on the order. Get your rhyming dictionaries into action.

For example, *In the Snow* or *Snowball Fight* (word pairs in no particular order):

blinking/sinking, sliding/colliding, slipping/tripping, calling/snowballing, throwing/snowing, chucking/ducking, lobbing/bobbing, catching/snatching, scheming/screaming, whamming/scramming, racing/chasing, dodging/splodging, rolling/bowling, conspiring/backfiring, winning/grinning, thrilling/down-hilling, spilling/chilling, aiming/exclaiming, crouching/ouching, scrunching/crunching, screaming/beaming, naming/blaming, yelling/pell-melling, freezing/sneezing, shivering/quivering, shouting/look-outing, falling/sprawling, trudging/sludging, roaming/homing.

- There should be enough there to construct something worthwhile – if not, I'll look for some more! The words are waiting just for me; it's only a matter of working at it.
- Not all of these will be useful, but the more I have to choose from the better.
- I haven't even considered near-rhymes yet.
- You can create verbs out of other parts of speech, e.g. down-hilling, pell-melling, look-outing.

Other poems in this volume that contain at least one internal rhyme:

The Man in the Moon Stayed Up Too Late by J. R. R. Tolkien (p. 35)
From a Railway Carriage by R. L. Stevenson (p. 38)
Snow by Jane Clarke (p. 73)
Chemistry Lesson by Elizabeth Ingate (p. 101)
Weather is Full of the Nicest Sounds by Aileen Fisher (p. 102)
The Great Water Giant by Ian Souter (p. 129)
The Clothes-Line by Charlotte Druitt Cole (p. 130)
Cool Cat and *Rockets* by Mike Jubb (pp. 42 and 78 respectively)

Rhyme, of course, is more often part of a pattern; I guess that's one reason for its popularity. Our eyes enjoy pattern, and so do our ears. But there are other, easier, ways of putting patterns into our poems in order to give them some unity. (This is explored in *A Poetry Teacher's Toolkit* Book 3, Ch. 1.)

*   *   *

There was a young (!) poet called Jubb
Whose near-rhymes were really quite good;
So he wrote them all down
Then went out on the town,
And recited them all in the pub.   C.D.

THE LITERACY HOUR: YEARS 3 AND 4

National Literacy Strategy objectives: Years 3 and 4

Year 3
- To distinguish between rhyming and non-rhyming poetry and comment on the impact of layout.
- To take account of the grammar and punctuation . . . when reading aloud.
- To continue the collection of new words from reading . . . and make use of them in reading and writing.

Year 4
- To identify different patterns of rhyme and verse in poetry.
- To reread own writing to check for coherence . . . and to suggest alternative constructions.
- To use phonic/spelling knowledge as a cue, together with graphic, grammatical and contextual knowledge, when reading unfamiliar texts.

Chosen poem

Monday Morning by John C. Head (p. 74)

Materials needed

Board or flipchart
Marker pens
Copies of the chosen poem (see 'Preparation')
Scissors, card, laminator (optional), envelopes
Pens, pencils, writing paper/books
Activity sheets (see 'Preparation')
Photocopiable sheet B (see 'Preparation')

Preparation

Make two enlarged copies of the poem.

Make copies of the activity sheets for each child, according to achievement level (photocopiable sheets 2a, 2b, 2c on pp. 65–67).

Make copies of photocopiable sheet B (p. 71) for Group 5.

Type out the poem on a computer using a 24-point font and print out several copies.

(One copy per pair or group of three should be enough.) Stick the copies onto card. (Laminate them if required for future use.) Cut them into their individual lines. Put each set of lines into separate envelopes to prevent them from getting mixed up and/or lost.

With the whole class

- Spend a few minutes talking about Monday mornings – ask some of the children to tell you what happens in their house on a Monday morning before they leave for school. If anyone's account is similar to the poem, encourage the class to discuss why a 'Monday morning rush' happens.
- Read the title of the poem and tell them that it's a bit different from many other poems but they will have no difficulty understanding the sequence of the poet's Monday morning!
- Share the poem with the children, making sure you use speed, expression and intonation to put across the various moods and tempo of each activity 'described'.
- Ask the children what they notice about this poem. Discuss some of the following points: the poem has only one noun ('school'), right at the end – do we still know what's happening? how?; the tempo moves from the reluctant slowness of getting up, to the frenzied scrambling into the car – how is this achieved?; what do the children notice about each line?; is there a rhyming pattern?; how did they feel when they heard the final two lines?; can they think of two rhyming words for a new final line that would continue the pattern?
- Look at some of the words and challenge the children to tell you others that rhyme with the lines you focus on, not necessarily connected with Monday morning activities. For example, for the line 'groping, soaping', they might suggest 'hoping', 'coping' or 'moping'. List their suggestions on the second enlarged copy beside the relevant line. Leave the sheet pinned to the wall with a pen on a string, and encourage the children to add more rhyming words to each line at other times of the day.
- Tell the children you're all going to write a class poem using some of the words from *Monday Morning*. Let the children choose a line and explain that you want them to use the words as the final words of two lines in a four-line verse. For example, if they choose 'mumbling, grumbling', their poem might read

> When it's Monday morning, we're in a rush
> And Dad is crossly mumbling.
> He always makes me hurry up,
> So I pay him back by grumbling.

- Write their ideas on the flipchart and redraft until everyone (or nearly everyone!) is happy with the poem. Put the final version on a clean page and leave it up for the group session.
- Before breaking into groups, share *Monday Morning* again, encouraging the children to join in.

Group and independent work (differentiated groups)

Group 1

Give the group the envelopes containing the lines of the poem on cards. Ask the children to work in pairs or as a group to experiment with putting some of the lines into a different order. (Give the number of cards according to achievement level.) Challenge them to make a new poem using their new order. If they want, let them write their poem in full sentences. Remind them it doesn't have to rhyme.

Group 2

Give out copies of activity sheets 2a (for lower achievers), 2b (for average achievers) and 2c (for higher achievers) and ask the children to complete them. Let them refer to the class poem if they need some support.

Group 3

Ask the group to make up some actions to go with *Monday Morning*. They should practise reciting the poem, putting their agreed actions to each line. When they are confident, arrange for them to give a class or school performance. (If possible, on a Monday morning!)

Group 4

Challenge the children to write a group poem called *Friday Evening*. Help them to brainstorm ideas for their poem and then draft and redraft until they are happy with their poem. Remind them it doesn't have to rhyme.

Group 5

Give out copies of photocopiable sheet B. Ask the children to use the 'Fish and Chips' phrases to make up some rhyming couplets (see activity above, p. 49). They could do this in pairs for support.

Plenary session (whole class)

- Ask a volunteer from the group that made up actions to the poem to teach them to the class. Have some fun reciting *Monday Morning* once again, putting the actions to the words.
- Did anyone think of new rhymes for any of the words in the poem? Were any added to the list? Spend a few minutes looking at the new words and see if they can be used to make up some extra lines for the poem.

THE LITERACY HOUR: YEARS 3 AND 4

National Literacy Strategy objectives: Years 5 and 6

Year 5
- To use the structures of poems read to write extensions based on these, e.g. additional verses, or substituting own words and ideas.
- To discuss, proofread and edit their own writing for clarity and correctness.
- To use a range of dictionaries and understand their purposes.

Year 6
- To produce revised poems for reading aloud individually.
- To adapt texts for particular readers and purposes.
- To experiment with language.

Chosen poem

Rockets by Mike Jubb (p. 78)

Materials needed

Board or flipchart
Coloured marker pens
Copies of the chosen poem (see 'Preparation')
Pens, pencils, drawing paper
Activity sheets (see 'Preparation')
Photocopiable sheet C (see 'Preparation')

Preparation

Enlarge two copies of the poem. Put one up for the whole-class session and cover it up, except for the title. (The other copy is for the group session.)

Write 'ROCKETS' several times vertically on the flipchart, as at the base of the poem.

Make copies of the activity sheets for each child, according to achievement level (photocopiable sheets 2aa, 2bb, 2cc on pp. 68–70).

Make copies of photocopiable sheet C (p. 72) for Group 5.

With the whole class

- Look at the title and ask the children what they think this poem could be about – don't give any hints that 'rockets' means fireworks rather than space travel. Jot down on the board key words for the children's ideas. Uncover the first line and ask a volunteer to read it. Did the children guess correctly about the subject of the poem?

- Share the poem with them, letting them follow the text as you read. When you have finished reading, ask the children whether they enjoyed the poem. Encourage them to say why or why not, referring to specific parts of the poem to support their opinions. Make sure that children who did not like the poem are listened to with respect.

- Spend some time exploring the poem in more detail. Can the children see a regular verse pattern? Explain that because there isn't one, the poem is an example of 'free verse'. Ask volunteers to show you some alliteration in the poem. (For example, 'rotten Roman candles', 'feeble fountains', 'drop down dead', 'cascades of colour', 'blue-black sky', 'frantic flight', 'snap-crackling sparkling star-streams'.) Can they find examples of assonance? (For example, 'real'/'keep'/'wheels' or 'fly'/'night'/'excitedly'.) What rhymes are there in the poem? (For example, 'dash'/'flash'/'crash'/'smash'/'splash'; 'sky'/'high'/'fly' or 'night'/'flight'/'height'.) Discuss which examples are internal rhymes.

- Share the poem again, encouraging the children to join in. Help them to recite the poem in a way that expresses the exciting and explosive nature of the rockets. Do they think the poet manages to capture the essence of what rockets are? Can they say how? (Or why not!)

- Brainstorm words associated with rockets and write the children's ideas on the flipchart. Focus on the flipchart where 'ROCKETS' has been written vertically. Help the children to match words that begin with any letter in 'rockets' to the columns. Together write an acrostic. Draft and redraft, encouraging the children to tell you what to write, until everybody is happy with the result. Write the final version on a clean page and leave it up for the group session.

Group and independent work (differentiated groups)

Group 1
Give out copies of activity sheets 2aa (for lower achievers), 2bb (for average achievers) and 2cc (for higher achievers). Let the children refer to the class poem for help if they need support.

Group 2
Give the enlarged copy of the poem to the children and ask them to use different colours to circle the rhyming words. They should use one colour for each 'rhyming family'.

Group 3
Help the children to make up a role play in which they are the rockets in Mike Jubb's poem. Discuss and practise what actions they could perform to put across the characteristics of rockets. When the role play has been agreed, recite the poem for the group as they perform the actions.

Group 4

Ask the children to use some of the brainstormed words associated with rockets to work together to write a group poem. They don't need to write an acrostic and their poem can be 'free verse'. Remind them to draft and redraft until they are happy with their poem.

Group 5

Give out photocopiable sheet C for the children to complete (see the 'Fish and Chips' activity above, p. 49). They could work in pairs for support.

Plenary session (whole class)

- Ask the children to give a recital of *Rockets* for you. Tell them that you are their audience and they should perform the poem in as exciting a way as possible.
- Did the class enjoy exploring and performing *Rockets*? Ask them to tell you why or why not.

SHEET 2a

Name _____

Write a poem about Monday mornings. You could use the words below to help you. Remember that your poem doesn't have to rhyme.

On Mondays, when we're in a _____

And Dad is crossly _____

He always makes me _____

So then I end up _____

hurry	mumbling	hurry up	moaning
rush	groaning	speed	grumbling

Read *Monday Morning* by John C. Head.

Choose two words from the poem and use them to write sentences about the Monday morning rush in your house:

_____

_____

Use a thesaurus to find alternative words for

moaning _____   scrubbing _____

_____   _____

SHEET 2b

Name _____

Write a poem about Monday mornings. You could use the words below to help you. Remember that your poem doesn't have to rhyme.

On Mondays, we're usually _____

And Mum is very _____

She always _____

I always _____

So then we end up _____

   hurrying   mumbling   shouting   hurry up   moan
   rush   groaning   speeding   late   cross   grumble

Read *Monday Morning* by John C. Head.

Choose three words from the poem and use them to write sentences about the Monday morning rush in your house:

_____

_____

_____

Use a thesaurus to find alternative words for

howling _____   muttering _____

_____   _____

crunching _____   rubbing _____

_____   _____

splashing _____   groaning _____

_____   _____

© Collette Drifte and Mike Jubb (2002) *A Poetry Teacher's Toolkit*, Book 2. London: David Fulton Publishers.

SHEET 2c

Name _____

Write a poem about Monday mornings. You could use the words below to help you. Remember that your poem doesn't have to rhyme.

Monday mornings are always _____

We usually _____

The bathroom _____

At breakfast we _____

And in the end _____

rush   groaning   speeding   late   cross   grumble

hurrying   mumbling   shouting   hurry up   moan

Read *Monday Morning* by John C. Head.

Choose four words from the poem and use them to write sentences about the Monday morning rush in your house:

_____

_____

_____

_____

Use a thesaurus to find alternative words for

sighing _____   glowering _____

_____   _____

cramming _____   dashing _____

_____   _____

splashing _____   groaning _____

_____   _____

SHEET 2aa

Name _____

Read *Rockets* by Mike Jubb, then complete this acrostic. You could use the words below to help you. Remember that your poem doesn't have to rhyme.

*R*oaring up to the sky,

*O*ver _____ they zoom;

*C*ascades of _____,

*K*ites of lights and sparkles!

*E*very one _____,

*T*hey zoom high and _____,

*S*plashing their colours across the sky.

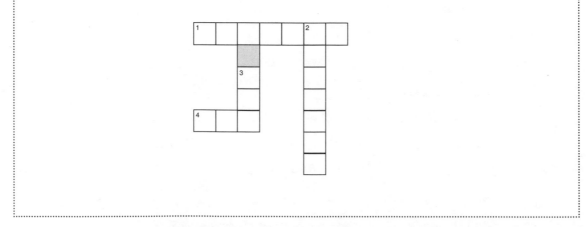

showers   brilliant   shooting   crash   swoosh   explosion

Now complete the crossword

Clues across

1. Something we burn on November 5th.

4. In *Rockets*, the poet talks of a 'blue-black _____'.

Clues down

2. Fireworks that zoom up to the sky.

3. A pretend man that sits on top of the bonfire.

© Collette Drifte and Mike Jubb (2002) *A Poetry Teacher's Toolkit*, Book 2. London: David Fulton Publishers.

SHEET 2bb

Name _____

Read *Rockets* by Mike Jubb, then complete this acrostic. You could use the words below to help you. Remember that your poem doesn't have to rhyme.

*R*ushing and zooming, up and

*O*ver the _____;

*C*olours that _____,

*K*ites of lights and sparkles!

*E*xploding as they _____,

*T*ill in the end, they _____,

*S*adly falling away and _____

clouds   shimmer   stars   sparkle   houses   zooming   fade   trickle

Now complete the crossword.

Clues across

2. A firework you hold in your hand.

4. In *Rockets*, the poet says that a rocket's 'first thunderous _____ attacks your ears'.

5. An effigy we burn on the bonfire.

Clues down

1. Where rockets shoot up to.

2. Something we eat on Bonfire Night.

3. The poet's favourite fireworks.

SHEET 2cc

Name _____

Read *Rockets* by Mike Jubb, then complete this acrostic. You could use some words from the poem to help you. Remember that your poem doesn't have to rhyme.

Rockets roaring and _____

On and up until _____;

Crashing and _____,

Kicking the clouds and _____

Exploding as they _____,

Till in the end, they _____,

Silently falling and _____.

Now complete the crossword.

Clues across

1. In *Rockets*, the poet speaks of 'exploding _____ of colour'.

3. Sausages or very loud fireworks.

4. In the poem, Mike Jubb speaks of 'A galaxy of _____ stars'.

6. Rockets do this just before they finish.

Clues down

1. In *Rockets*, the poet says that Roman _____ are 'rotten'.

2. They twinkle in the sky at night.

3. We burn this on 5th November.

5. An effigy burned on the fire on November 5th.

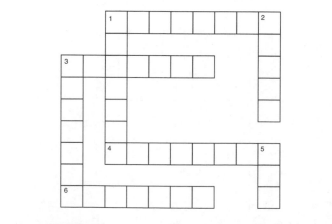

PHOTOCOPIABLE SHEET B

Name _____

Read these 'Fish and Chips' phrases:

Mum and Dad   Up and Down   Chalk and Cheese

Left and Right   Cat and Mouse   Laugh and Cry

Bread and Jam   Coat and Hat

Now use them to make up some rhyming couplets. Two have been done for you:

Mum and Dad   Chalk and Cheese

Aren't so bad   Make me sneeze

Up and Down   Left and Right

_____   _____

Cat and Mouse   Laugh and Cry

_____   _____

Bread and Jam   Coat and Hat

_____   _____

PHOTOCOPIABLE SHEET C

Name _____

Write a word to go with each of these to make assonance. Your words should be linked in some way. Some have been done for you:

Shout / Frown   Thunder / Rumble   Pond / Swan

Chair / _____   Laugh / _____   High / _____

Tremble / _____   Grass / _____   Windy / _____

Now make a couplet for each pair of words:

_____   _____

_____   _____

_____   _____

_____   _____

_____   _____

_____   _____

Snow

Jane Clarke

White snow, bright snow,
Silent in the night snow.
Crystal petal snowflakes

    s
     e
      t t
      l e

Sparkle in the light snow.

Deep snow, heaped snow,
Leap about and sweep snow.
Snowdrifts, snowfalls,
snowmen, snowballs,
Hands and feet aglow snow.

Cold snow, old snow,
Melting as you hold snow.
Icy, slushy,
Dirty, mushy,
Time for you to go snow.

Monday Morning

John C. Head

Moaning, groaning,
mumbling, grumbling,
glowering, showering,
rubbing, scrubbing,
washing, sploshing,
groping, soaping,
howling, towelling,
splashing, dashing,
muttering, buttering,
crunching, munching,
sighing, tying,
brushing, rushing,
cramming, slamming,
and off to
school.

Roses are Red

Anon.

Roses are red,
violets are blue,
most poems rhyme
but this one doesn't.

John Bun

Anon.

Here lies John Bun:
He was killed by a gun.
His name wasn't Bun, it was Wood;
But Wood wouldn't rhyme with gun, and Bun would.

Five Little Owls

Anon.

Five little owls in an old elm-tree,
Were fluffy and puffy as owls can be,
They were blinking and winking with big round eyes
At the big round moon that hung in the sky.
As I passed beneath, I heard one say,
'There'll be mouse for supper, there will, today!'
Then all of them hooted, 'Tu-whit, Tu-whoo!
Yes, mouse for supper, Hoo hoo, Hoo hoo!'

Yeti

Paul Bright

I claim with confidence, I've met
Most creatures in the alphabet.
I've hunted them with noose or net,
From aardvark, ape and avocet,
Through musk-ox, moose and marmoset,
To xiphias and zebra, yet
It is to my intense regret
I haven't seen a Yeti yet.

I've trekked by mule with my machete,
Getting chilly, mucky, sweaty,
And, though you may call it petty,
Still I've never found a Yeti.

I've searched regions dry and wet.
I've scoured the plateau of Tibet.
I've studied Yeti etiquette,
Seen things I think a Yeti's ate,
And though I'm not the sort to fret,
I'm really getting quite upset
That I've not seen or smelt or met
Or found or caught a Yeti yet!

Bare Back Riding

Mike Jubb

I've ridden a New Forest pony,
I've ridden a camel too;
I've ridden a wonky donkey,
And a llama in darkest Peru;
I've ridden a mule in Morocco,
But there's one thing I don't recommend:
That's riding a hedgehog naked,
Cos it don't half hurt your rear end.

Rockets

Mike Jubb

Rockets are the only *real* fireworks!

You can keep your Catherine wheels that stick.
You can stick your rotten Roman candles and
your feeble fountains that hiss and splutter,
pretty-pretty-tinkle-silver snow-storms that
                                                    drop down dead.
Give me rockets instead!

Rockets get off to a flying start.
They dart and dash,
        they flash
                crash
                    smash
                and splash their exploding cascades of colour
on the blue-black sky.
Hurtling high,
rockets fly furiously.
They zip,
    and rip into the night, excitedly,
in a swooshing frantic flight, ready to burst, until,
                    at their height,
the first thunderous crack attacks your ears, and
a galaxy of shooting stars spreads in all directions.

Rockets whistle and scream
            and send teeming, snap-crackling sparkling star-streams
of cosmic red, green nebula and galactic gold.

Rockets **(continued)**

On a cold, bright November night,
      you can keep your fountains that fizz.
      Half-hearted fireworks.

Give me the daring, sky-tearing whoosh and whiz of

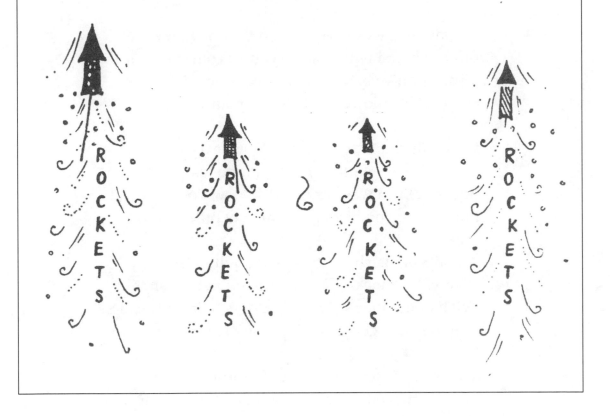

Henry the Eighth Doesn't Visit Relate

Emma Woodward, age 9

(Rupert House School, Henley-on-Thames)

Catherine of Aragon, I **don't** wish you were here,
Speak up, I can't hear you, your reply isn't clear.
I know that you want to stay here with me
But you must go back to Spain, over the sea.
You won't give me an heir and I need a small boy
So I'm packing you off as I'm **not** full of joy!

For my next wife, I've wed you, Anne Boleyn,
But I'm bored with you, so you've committed a sin!
I'll say you've betrayed me with lovers in bed,
So now I'm allowed to chop off your head!

Now, which pretty wench will be next in my line?
I fancy Jane Seymour, yes, you'll do just fine!
But childbirth was hard, and so now you are dead
But at least you have given me my little son, Ed!

A political match might suit me quite well
With you, Anne of Cleves, but you never can tell,
I've had my four starters, I've done with this course,
I think I shall get yet another divorce.

My penultimate wife is you, Kathryn Howard,
But I'll chop off your head so don't be a coward!
For you have been naughty and seen other men,
If I chop off your head, you can't do it again!

My last but not least wife is you, Katherine Parr,
What a lucky and fortunate girl that you are!
You weren't divorced and your head is still on,
But only because I am dead and am gone!

Changing My Little Brother's Nappy

Lisa Rhodes

(Peel Common Junior School, Gosport)

When I change my little brother's nappy,
He always wiggles and is always happy;
But not me. I mean his nappy leaks;
When you take it off it totally reaks.

When I change my little brother's diaper,
He always wiggles and is always hyper;
Mum never does it. She always makes me!
The stuff inside looks like his tea!

3 Sounds Good

Featured poems

Chemistry Lesson by Elizabeth Ingate
Weather is Full of the Nicest Sounds by Aileen Fisher
Pleasant Sounds by John Clare
The Isle is Full of Noises by William Shakespeare
Camilla Caterpillar by Mike Jubb
From *Rain in Summer* by H. W. Longfellow
I Dunno, Anon.
I Asked the Maid in Dulcet Tone, Anon.

'The crown of literature is poetry. It is its end and aim. It is the sublimest activity of the human mind. It is the achievement of beauty and delicacy. The writer of prose can only step aside when the poet passes.' (W. Somerset Maugham)

There is a range of 'sound effects' that a poet can employ in order to add texture and interest to a poem. The golden rule with all of them is: **don't overdo it**.

Used in moderation, devices such as assonance, onomatopoeia and alliteration can add to the power and the musicality of poetry. But, if they're hammered home with a heavy hand, they hardly help. The device itself can become the focus, a distraction. It can draw attention to itself, like strings of gaudy jewellery hanging round a beautiful neck. (See Chapter 4 for more about similes.)

Assonance

Assonance is the rhyming of vowel sounds (but not consonants) in nearby words: such as in 'time' and 'light'. There is some overlap with near-rhymes here, because assonance is also the use of identical consonants with different vowels: such as in chilled/called/fold/mild/failed/hurled.

Pleasant Sounds by John Clare (p. 103)

- There are examples of onomatopoeia: 'rustling' and 'rustle', 'crumping', 'halloos', 'whizzing', 'patter' and 'pattering'.
- Examples of vowel assonance include: leaves/feet; cat-ice/wood-rides; rustling/

rushing/thunder; brown/ground (near-rhyme); fall/acorn. Some of these may have been happy coincidences, but, deliberate or not, they add to the musicality of Clare's verse. He was a natural.

On the other hand, I'm sure that the assonance of 'thirsty earth', at the end of Ian Souter's *The Great Water Giant* (p. 129), is designed as a subtle finish to a well-crafted poem.

 ## WRITING ACTIVITY: Introducing assonance

Ask the children to write sentences that include at least two, but no more than three, of the words below. However, the words must come from different columns. Children should be allowed, in fact encouraged, to add 'ing', 'ed' or other endings to some of the words as appropriate.

treat	wheel	peep	seen	dream	feed	thief	seek
feet	feel	sleep	lean	stream	greed	beneath	week
beat	heel	creep	green	scream	lead	chief	weak
cheat	steal	deep	queen	team	need	teeth	speak
heat	meal	leap	jeans	steam	speed	believe	cheek
meet	real	sheep	mean	cream	freed	underneath	beak

So, I'm looking for sentences such as:

> Parent birds are feeding hungry beaks.
> A thief came on creeping feet.
> I needed to speak to the chief.
> I was feeling all steamed up.
> The monster had green teeth.

Each sentence that the children produce in this way is potentially the first line of a separate poem. **Not** a rhyming poem this time please, nor one liberally scattered with assonances of the 'ee' kind. Just the start of a piece of free verse, following the lead of the opening sentence, which will have its own natural rhythm (not meter) to set the tone.

If you build up a bank of word lists like this one, you'll have an endless supply of kick-off material. I know it's yet another bit of preparation – so why not ask a loved-one or a friendly parent. Many adults, who may never read poetry, love word challenges. And you work harder than they do anyway. (For more about free verse, see *A Poetry Teacher's Toolkit* Book 3, Ch. 2.)

Onomatopoeia

Onomatopoeia is the imitation of sounds in word form. The onomatopoeic activities in *A Poetry Teacher's Toolkit* Book 1 are fun, but are not really what onomatopoeia is about in poetry. In poetry, it doesn't exist for its own sake, but to add a little 'sound colour' to a piece where appropriate. It might be comparable to where, in a symphony, there is a single beat where one 'ting' on the triangle is just right. (See also *A Poetry Teacher's Toolkit* Book 1, Ch. 2 and Ch. 3.)

WRITING ACTIVITY: Crash Bang Tinkle

As a stepping stone from the totally onomatopoeic pieces (in *A Poetry Teacher's Toolkit* Book 1), to a more subtle use of this figure of speech, poems could be written for contexts such as:

> a sweet factory;
> Robot World;
> a building site;
> an adventure park;
> an onomatopoeic walk to school

The children can begin by making a list of likely words. Lists are great starters for poems. Gradually, they will learn to add linking words and how to structure. You could always suggest a structure to build on, but if children can come up with a pattern of their own, so much the better.

> As I was walking to school today,
> a motorbike whizzed past;
> nnnnnnnnneeeeeooooooooooooooowwwwwww!

> As I was walking to school today,
> a car braked hard at the traffic lights;
> screeeeeeeeeeeeeeeeeeeeeeeeeech!

> As I was walking to school today,
> a man was hammering nails;
> Bang! Bang! Bang! Bang! Ooooowww!   M.J.

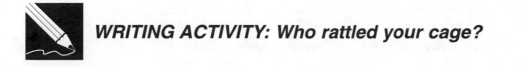

WRITING ACTIVITY: Who rattled your cage?

Ask the children to bring in action pictures from magazines, or home photo albums. They have to write a single sentence describing the action, but they must include an onomatopoeic word. Experiment with how you use this sentence, but one way would be to take the pictures away after the initial stimulation, then make the children swap their sentences with someone from another group, and use their new one as the first line of a poem in free verse.

Weather is Full of the Nicest Sounds by Aileen Fisher (p. 102)

Let's get the grumbles out of the way first. I HATE 'nicest'! Ask the children to suggest better alternatives. Get them to say the sentences out loud.

'Weather is full of fascinating sounds'
'Weather is full of interesting sounds'
'Weather is full of percussive sounds'

or simply

'Weather is full of sounds'

I don't care much for 'a mouse in her house' either. Having got all that off my chest, this poem is a riot of onomatopoeia; about a third of the words are onomatopoeic. Normally, it's better to use figures of speech in moderation except, as here, when you're making a feature of it (many more onomatopoeic words can be found in *Roget's Thesaurus*).

The rhyme scheme of this poem looks chaotic:

(A B C B A D E D F G E G F H H H I I J K K J L L J J)

but it works wonderfully, and makes for a particularly musical piece. To sum up, this is a super poem for performance (see *A Poetry Teacher's Toolkit* Book 4).

Alliteration

Alliteration refers to words that begin with the same sound, not necessarily the same letter, e.g. one wonderful woman with nine naughty knights!

Alliteration should be used
in moderation, and not abused.

A little alliteration

A little alliteration
like 'lizards licking liquorice'
is a super sound sensation
so snortsomeful and snickerish;
children chewing chocolate chips
are standing at the station,
and taking turns to try to teach
a little alliteration.   M.J.

Again, it depends on the type of poem being written. If you want the children to make a deliberate feature of alliteration, such as in a tongue-twister, then by all means let them try to squeeze in as much as they can.

When wizards and witches want windier weather
When witches and wizards want wind with a whiz
We waggle our wands and we wangle our whooshers
We wind up our woomsticks and wheeeeeeeeeee . . . there it is.   M.J.

I hope this tongue-twister demonstrates something of the craft of writing poetry. This verse wasn't written – it was constructed, put together, assembled. It contains not only a great deal of alliteration, but also rhyme, meter, assonance, onomatopoeia and new words. For all its triviality, it is the result of going over the piece again and again until I decided it was the best I could do with that idea. (For more about creating new words, see *A Poetry Teacher's Toolkit* Book 4.)

WRITING ACTIVITY: Introducing alliteration

Make up sentences that the children must finish off with an alliterative word or phrase. For example: My mum made me . . . (mow the lawn; mop the floor; make the beds; miss my bus; mad).

If a child or group can come up with enough of these, it's worth being on the lookout for a chance to put some together.

My mum made me miss my bus,
My mum made me mop the floor,
My mum made me make the beds,
My mum made me mow the lawn.

My mum makes me mad.   M.J.

Other starters: Fiona found; Hector hates; David doesn't; Cartoon cats can; Make your own up.

WRITING ACTIVITY: Towards tongue-twisting

For this one, the children need to do some word collecting first. Get them to choose one letter of the alphabet, or allocate one to them. (It's probably a good idea to ban certain letters, such as 'q', 'x' and 'z'.) Then give them a list of categories, such as:

a first name; a surname; a verb; an adverb; a colour; an animal; a country; a town or city; a location (shop, library, park, etc.); a food; an occupation; a sport; a famous person; a popular product; an item of clothing; an emotion.

The children must think of one word in each of, say, five of the categories (including a verb) beginning with the chosen letter. For example, Mike (a first name); marmalade (a food); monkey (an animal); mix (a verb); miserable (an emotion).

Then they have to work all the words into one alliterative sentence, e.g. Mike mixed the miserable monkey's marmalade (with maggots).

or

Choose just one of the above categories. Think of one word that begins with the chosen letter, and brainstorm a few alliterative words to go with it.

Category: Town. Specifically: Bognor. Possible words: beach; bucket; boat; bathers; balloon; Bob; bought; bounce; blue.

e.g. Bob bought a boat in Bognor

More able children might try a rhyme.

Bob bought a bucket in Bognor,
Bob bought bathers too;
Bob went bouncing down the beach
Like a blinking kangaroo. (or even 'bangaroo')   M.J.

However, much of the time, alliteration needs to be deployed with subtlety. In those cases, it shouldn't attract attention to itself, and away from the poem, by overuse. The effect should be subliminal – on the ear but not on the conscious mind. Of course (not being known for their subtlety) once children learn about alliteration as a writing device, they may understandably go over the top.

It's horses for courses, but when used inappropriately it can be like the difference between subtle make-up and a clown's face. So children need to learn **how** to be subtle. And the best way to learn is to read and hear as much good practice as possible.

Many of the poems featured in this volume (and the others in this series), offer good examples of controlled alliteration, e.g.:

'Bunsens burning' in *Chemistry Lesson* by Elizabeth Ingate
'the crumping of cat-ice' in John Clare's *Pleasant Sounds*
'Sounds, and sweet airs' from *The Tempest*

*   *   *

I spent lots of time
Making up rhymes, (well – near-ones, anyway)
With assonance and alliteration.
But I just couldn't do it (before the deadline . . .)
I guess I just blew it. In future
I'll know my own station.   C.D.

THE LITERACY HOUR: YEARS 3 AND 4

National Literacy Strategy objectives: Years 3 and 4

Year 3
- To recognise . . . alliteration and other patterns of sound that create effects.
- To take account of the grammar and punctuation . . . when reading aloud.
- To continue the collection of new words from reading . . . and make use of them in reading and writing.

Year 4
- To write poems, experimenting with different styles and structures.
- To . . . work on expressive language in . . . poetry.
- To use phonic/spelling knowledge as a cue, together with graphic, grammatical and contextual knowledge, when reading unfamiliar texts.

Chosen poem

Weather is Full of the Nicest Sounds by Aileen Fisher (p. 102)

Materials needed

Board or flipchart
Marker pens
Enlarged copy of the chosen poem (see 'Preparation')
Musical instruments such as percussion, wind and string
Old comics, card, scissors, 'feely' bag, counters or tokens
Noun picture cards, letter tiles, feely bag
Activity sheets (see 'Preparation')
Situation cards (see 'Preparation')
Cassette recorder and blank cassette
Pens, pencils, writing books

Preparation

Enlarge the poem and cover it up except for the title.

Cut out the onomatopoeic words from the comics and stick them onto card. Put them into a feely bag.

Put the letter tiles into the feely bag.

Make copies of the activity sheets for each child, according to achievement level (photocopiable sheets 3a, 3b, 3c on pp. 95–97).

Make a set of situation cards for Group 5. For example, *In a shopping mall*; *In the High Street*; *In the swimming pool*; *In the football stadium*, etc.

With the whole class

- Ask a volunteer to read the title and then ask the children what they think the poem might be about. Can they suggest some words that hint at the sounds of weather? List their ideas on the board and leave them up. Don't mention the term 'onomatopoeia' at this stage and leave it until later to explore their suggestions for onomatopoeia or alliteration.

- Uncover the poem and share it with the children using tone, tempo and expression to convey the idea in each line. When you have finished, ask them whether they enjoyed the poem. Encourage them to tell you why or why not.

- Look at the suggestions made by the children at the beginning of the session. Were any of their words in the poem? If any of their words suggest weather other than thunderstorms, tell them that you'll come back to those words later.

- Look at the 'sound' word in each line of the poem and invite the children to suggest when it might be used. For example, 'pounds' could be for a gale-force wind, 'splishes' for gentle rain and 'mumbles' for distant thunder.

- Ask the children what these words are trying to do. Tease out that most of them are conveying the sound made by thundery weather. Ask whether they know what name we have for these words? Write 'onomatopoeia' on the board and read it to them. Spend a few minutes explaining what onomatopoeic words are and why we use them in poetry.

- Can the children tell you what weather is *not* explored in the poem? Agree one type – such as a dull, foggy day, or a still, snowy day – and brainstorm words associated with it. Encourage the children to suggest or make up onomatopoeic words that convey the mood of the chosen weather. If there were any appropriate words suggested at the beginning of the session, explore these and decide whether they are onomatopoeic, or can be made so.

- Together, write a class poem in the style of Aileen Fisher's, starting with the line

      Snowy / sunny / rainy, etc. weather is full
      of the nicest sounds

- Draft and redraft until (almost) everyone is satisfied with their work. Write the final version on a clean sheet of paper, or section of the board and leave it up for the group session. (For more detail about onomatopoeia, see *A Poetry Teacher's Toolkit* Book 4, Ch. 3.)

Group and independent work (differentiated groups)

Group 1

Give out the musical instruments and have some fun 'orchestrating' *Weather is Full of the Nicest Sounds*. Experiment with the different instruments for the different words until the group is happy with its work. Practise playing and reciting. You could either split the group into 'players or sayers', or help everyone to play and say. (This may need to be done away from the main classroom.)

Group 2

Give out copies of activity sheets 3a (for lower achievers), 3b (for average achievers) and 3c (for higher achievers), and ask the children to complete them. Let them refer to the chosen poem or the class poem for support.

Group 3

Put the noun picture cards face down on the table, together with the feely bag containing the letter tiles. Give out the pencils and paper or writing books. Ask the children to work as a group, taking turns to turn over a noun picture card and take out two letter tiles. They should make up onomatopoeic words beginning with one of the letters that would be associated with the picture. For example, if they took out the letters 'c' and 'm', and turned over the picture of a cow, they might come up with 'chompersome' and 'moombling'. If writing their words is difficult, they could record them onto a cassette.

Group 4

Give the counters or tokens and the feely bag full of onomatopoeic words to the group. Let them play a game where each child takes a card out of the bag and reads the word aloud. They then have to suggest something associated with the word and, if the others agree that it's a good example, they win a token. For example, 'SCREEEEEECHHHHH' could be a car's brakes, or a cat's reaction to seeing a dog. The child with the highest number of tokens at the end of the game is the winner.

Group 5

Give the cassette recorder, blank cassette and situation cards to the group. Ask them to make up onomatopoeic words that are appropriate to each setting (see activity above, p. 84). They should record their words on the blank cassette and, if possible, write them down. Challenge them to make up sentences using the onomatopoeic words. Can they make their sentences into a poem?

Plenary session (whole class)

- Ask someone from each group to share with the class what their task was. If they made up new onomatopoeic words, invite the other children to guess what each new word is describing.
- Share *Weather is Full of the Nicest Sounds* once more, encouraging the children to join in. If anyone wrote a poem, tell them that you will display it for the others to read.

THE LITERACY HOUR: YEARS 5 AND 6

National Literacy Strategy objectives: Years 5 and 6

Year 5
- To express their views about a . . . poem, identifying specific words or phrases to support their viewpoint.
- To discuss, proofread and edit their own writing for clarity and correctness.
- To explore onomatopoeia.

Year 6
- To contribute constructively to shared discussion about literature, responding to and building on the views of others.
- To adapt texts for particular readers and purposes.
- To experiment with language.

Chosen poem

Chemistry Lesson by Elizabeth Ingate (p. 101)

Materials needed

Enlarged copy of the chosen poem (see 'Preparation')
Board or flipchart
Marker pens
Large sheet of paper if a flipchart is not being used
Cassette recorder/player and blank cassette
Copies of the chosen poem for each child in Group 2
Pens, pencils, writing paper/books
Drawing paper, coloured pencils or markers
Activity sheets (see 'Preparation')
Sentence cards (see 'Preparation')

Preparation

Enlarge the poem.

Make copies of the activity sheets for each child, according to achievement level (photocopiable sheets 3aa, 3bb, 3cc on pp. 98–100).

Make cards with incomplete alliterative sentences such as *Fred Foster found a few* —, *Cheerful Charlie chased* — , *Stephen and Sally swapped* — .

With the whole class

- Tell the children you're going to read them a poem called *Chemistry Lesson*, by Elizabeth Ingate. Can they tell you what a chemistry lesson is? Does anybody have a chemistry set at home? Does anybody have an older sibling who does chemistry lessons at their school?

- Before you read the poem, ask the children what they think it might be about. Jot down on the board key words from their suggestions to refer to later.

- Share the poem with the children letting them follow the text as you read. When you have finished, ask them whether they enjoyed the poem. Can they say why or why not? Ask them to refer to specific words or phrases to support their opinions.

- Look at the key words jotted on the board at the beginning of the session. How accurate were the children's guesses?

- Are there any words or phrases in the poem that they don't understand? For example, 'Bunsens burning' or 'Test tubes'. Help them to work out the meaning of these from the rest of the text.

- Spend some time exploring the poem in more detail. What do the children notice about the first two lines? (For example, rhymes and onomatopoeia – 'fizz' and 'Whiz'; alliteration and onomatopoeia – 'bubble' and 'bang'.) Can they point out examples of onomatopoeia? (For example, 'shuffling', 'ruffling', 'scraping', 'slamming', 'clinking', 'clanking', 'gurgling', etc.) Are there examples of alliteration? (For example, 'clinking, clanking', '. . . boiling, Bunsens burning', 'Sparks are spraying' or 'Pens at paper'.) Are they able to find assonance? (For example, 'Murmurs gurgling', 'Churning/ turning . . . working', 'rising. Silence!') Who calls 'Silence!' in the poem? Why? Where are the doors slamming? Is there a difference between the beginning and the end of the poem in terms of noise or sounds? If so what? Are there other times that parts of this poem could be used to describe, either in a school or elsewhere? For example, in a garage workshop or in a factory.

- Share the poem once again, telling the children to think about the ideas they have just explored. Did they enjoy the poem more on the second reading? Can they say why or why not?

- What other lessons would make good subjects for a sound poem? For example a football session or a cookery lesson. List the children's ideas on the board and ask them for words that could be used for each one. Write their ideas under each heading and leave them up for the group session.

- Choose one topic and together make some sentences that could be combined in poem form. Draft and redraft until everyone is satisfied, then write the final version on a large sheet of paper. Leave this pinned up for the group session.

Group and independent work (differentiated groups)

Group 1

Ask the group to choose a lesson, either one of those suggested during the whole-class session, or another one, and write a group poem. Remind them it does not have to rhyme and that they should brainstorm words and phrases before they start. Tell them they could use the words on the board for support if they wish. Encourage them to draft and redraft before deciding the final version. Let them record their poem onto a cassette.

Group 2
Give the children copies of the poem and activity sheets 3aa (for lower achievers), 3bb (for average achievers) and 3cc (for higher achievers). Ask them to share the poem as a group before completing their activity sheets.

Group 3
Ask the group to make a play about the lesson in the poem. Encourage them to use language and actions that convey the atmosphere of the poem.

Group 4
Ask the children to illustrate *Chemistry Lesson*, trying to include most of the things that Elizabeth Ingate describes in the poem. They should then write captions or sentences to go with their pictures.

Group 5
Put the sentence cards face down on the table. Ask the children to each take a card in turn. They should complete the sentence with an alliterative word or phrase (see activity above, p. 87). Challenge the children to make up their own sentences with alliteration.

Plenary session (whole class)

- Did anyone discover something new about *Chemistry Lesson* while they were working in their groups? Ask them to share their ideas with the class. Did the children who wrote new poems find it easy? Can they say why or why not?
- Ask the group that made a play from the poem to give a class performance. Did they include most of the ideas in the poem? Did they find it difficult to move from a poem to a play? Can they say how their work could be improved? What would they do differently if they had to do the activity again?

SHEET 3a

Name _____

Read Aileen Fisher's *Weather is Full of the Nicest Sounds*.

Write a poem in the same style called *Windy Days*. You could use the words below for help.

Windy days are full
of the nicest sounds:

they _____
and _____
and _____
and _____
I have to say a windy day
Makes me _____.

swish   whoosh   howl   roar   hum   whisper   rustle

Write some words that describe the sounds made by

rain _____   _____

hail _____   _____

snow _____   _____

SHEET 3b

Name _____

Read Aileen Fisher's *Weather is Full of the Nicest Sounds*.

Write a poem in the same style called *Windy Days*. You could use some of the words below for help. Try to find some of your own, too.

Windy days are full
of the nicest sounds:

they _____
and _____
and _____
and _____
and _____
and _____
I have to say a windy day
Makes me _____
and _____.

    swish   howl   roar   whisper   rustle

Write some words that describe the sounds made by

snow _____   _____

hail _____   _____

rain _____   _____

SHEET 3c

Name _____

Read Aileen Fisher's *Weather is Full of the Nicest Sounds*.

Write a poem in the same style called *Windy Days*.

Windy days are full
of the nicest sounds:

they _____

and _____

and _____

and _____

and _____

and _____

and _____

I have to say a windy day

Makes me _____

and _____

and _____ .

Write some words that describe the sounds made by

hail _____ _____ _____ _____

snow _____ _____ _____ _____

rain _____ _____ _____ _____

SHEET 3aa

Name _____

Read *Chemistry Lesson* by Elizabeth Ingate.

Match each example from the poem to the right form. One has been done for you.

alliteration ————————→ Clinking, clanking,

onomatopoeia   shuffling, ruffling

alliteration   ruffling, gurgling

rhyme   turning, working

assonance   Pens at paper

Decide what these onomatopoeic words could be describing:

Greebling _____

Floshing _____

Clugelling _____

SHEET 3bb

Name _____

Read *Chemistry Lesson* by Elizabeth Ingate.

Match each example from the poem to the right form. One has been done for you. Be careful – some examples fit more than one category!

alliteration ————————▶	Clinking, clanking,
onomatopoeia	fizz, Whiz
alliteration	slamming, gurgling
rhyme	Clinking, clanking
assonance	Bunsens burning
onomatopoeia	Murmurs gurgling
alliteration	shuffling, ruffling
rhyme	Sparks are spraying
assonance	Churning, working

Decide what these onomatopoeic words could be describing:

Twarfling _____

Shloobling _____

Gragging _____

Wiffling _____

SHEET 3cc

Name _____

Read *Chemistry Lesson* by Elizabeth Ingate.

Match each example from the poem to the right form. One has been done for
you. Be careful – some examples fit more than one category!

alliteration ————————→ Clinking, clanking,

                        Clinking   onomatopoeia

assonance   Bunsens burning

                        gurgling   alliteration

onomatopoeia   Sparks are spraying

                    rising. Silence   rhyme

rhyme   Pens at paper

                      Churning   assonance

assonance   shuffling, ruffling

                      fizz, Whiz   alliteration

alliteration   Murmurs gurgling

                 Churning, working   onomatopoeia

Decide what these onomatopoeic words could be describing:

Chickling _____

Foothing _____

Quagging _____

Sheesling _____

Detching_____

Chemistry Lesson

Elizabeth Ingate

Bubble, fizz,
Whiz and bang –
A Cauldron full
Of marbled sound.
Feet are shuffling,
Paper ruffling,
Stool legs scraping.
Doors are slamming.
Listen to the
Coughing, choking,
Clinking, clanking,
Test tubes boiling,
Bunsens burning.
Sparks are spraying,
Rising, falling,
Landing in a glow of red.
Listen to the
Murmurs gurgling,
Whispers growing,
Voices rising.
'Silence!'
Concentration,
Eyes are watching,
All ears listening.
Pens at paper
Heads bent low,
Brains in action,
Churning, turning,
All are working.

Weather is Full of the Nicest Sounds

Aileen Fisher

Weather is full
of the nicest sounds:
it sings
and rustles
and pings
and pounds
and hums
and tinkles
and strums
and twangs
and whishes
and sprinkles
and splishes
and bangs
and mumbles
and grumbles
and rumbles
and flashes
and CRASHES.
I wonder
if thunder
frightens a bee,
a mouse in her house,
a bird in a tree,
a bear
or a hare
or a fish in the sea?
Not *me*!

Pleasant Sounds

John Clare

The rustling of leaves under the feet in the woods
   and under hedges;
The crumping of cat-ice and snow down wood-rides,
   narrow lanes and every street causeway;
Rustling through a wood or rather rushing, while the
   wind halloos in the oak-top like thunder;
The rustle of birds' wings startled from their nests or
   flying unseen into the bushes;
The whizzing of larger birds overhead in a wood,
   such as crows, puddocks, buzzards;
The trample of robins and woodlarks on the brown
   leaves, and the patter of squirrels on the green moss;
The fall of an acorn on the ground, the pattering of
   nuts on the hazel branches as they fall from ripeness;
The flirt of the groundlark's wing from the stubbles –
   how sweet such pictures on dewy mornings,
   when the dew flashes from its brown feathers!

The Isle is Full of Noises

William Shakespeare

The isle is full of noises,
Sounds, and sweet airs, that give delight and
hurt not.
Sometimes a thousand twangling instruments
Will hum about mine ears; and sometimes
voices,
That, if I then had waked after a long sleep,
Will make me sleep again.

Camilla Caterpillar

Mike Jubb

Camilla Caterpillar kept a caterpillar killer-cat.
A caterpillar killer categorically she kept.
But alas the caterpillar killer-cat attacked Camilla
As Camilla Caterpillar catastrophically slept.

Extract from *Rain in Summer*

H. W. Longfellow

How beautiful is the rain!
After the dust and heat,
In the broad and fiery street,
In the narrow lane,
How beautiful is the rain!

How it clatters along the roofs,
Like the tramp of hoofs!
How it gushes and struggles out
From the throat of the overflowing spout!

Across the window-pane
It pours and pours;
And swift and wide,
With muddy tide,
Like a river down the gutter roars
The rain, the welcome rain!

I Dunno

Anon.

I sometimes think I'd rather crow
And be a rooster, than to roost
And be a crow. But I dunno.
A rooster he can roost also,
Which don't seem fair when crows can't crow,
Which may help some. Still, I dunno.

Crows should be glad of one thing though;
Nobody thinks of eating crow,
While roosters are good enough
For anyone, unless they're tough.

There's lots of tough old roosters though,
And anyway a crow can't crow,
So mebby roosters stand more show.
It looks that way. But, I dunno.

I Asked the Maid in Dulcet Tone

Anon.

I asked the maid in dulcet tone
To order me a buttered scone.
The silly girl has been and gone
And ordered me a buttered scone.

4 It's Like This . . .

Featured poems

The Great Water Giant by Ian Souter
The Clothes-Line by Charlotte Druitt Cole
Grandpa by Berlie Doherty
The Heron by Ted Hughes
The Windmill by H. W. Longfellow
Extract from *Indian Summer* by Emily Dickinson
The Flint by Christina Rossetti
Boats Sail on the Rivers by Christina Rossetti
If I Knew, Anon.

'Writing is like driving a car at night. You can only see as far as the headlights, but you make the whole trip that way.' (E. L. Doctorow)

Simile

Simile: a figure of speech involving the comparison of one thing with another thing of a different kind, as an illustration or ornament.

Similes usually, but not necessarily, contain the word 'like' or 'as'. I'm going to start a collection of similes without either of those words – so far, I have got one:

Shall I compare thee to a summer's day?
Thou art more lovely and more temperate. (Shakespeare)

There are many similes that are also clichés. Obviously, these are not the ones we want children to use in their creative writing, unless they're going to make a deliberate feature of them. Here's a few:

like a house on fire; like clockwork; like death warmed up; like something the cat brought in; like two peas in a pod; like it was going out of fashion; like a bat out of hell; like flogging a dead horse; like a cat on a hot tin roof; work like a beaver (Trojan); like a fish out of water; like a dog with a bone; go (run) like the wind; like looking for a needle in a haystack; like a shot in the arm; sleep like a log.

And then there's:

> quiet as a mouse; strong as an ox; mad as a hatter; cunning (sly) as a fox; innocent as a lamb; neat as a pin; nutty as a fruitcake; clear as day; plain as the nose on your face; pleased as Punch; pretty as a picture; quick as a wink; right as rain; sick as a dog (parrot); smart as a whip; soft as silk; snug as a bug in a rug; tight as a drum; thick as thieves; busy as a bee; clean as a whistle; clear as a bell; cool as a cucumber; bald as a coot; crazy as a coot; dead as a doornail; drunk as a skunk; dry as dust; dull as ditchwater; easy as pie; flat as a pancake; free as a bird; fresh as a daisy; bold as brass; large as life; tough as old boots; thin as a rake; poor as a church mouse; daft as a brush and wet as a scrubber; slow as a snail; blind as a bat; deaf as a post; slippery as an eel; hairy as an ape; sweet as honey; fit as a fiddle; high as a kite; wriggly as a worm; warm as toast; slimy as a snake; smooth as a baby's bottom; beautiful as a butterfly; old as time; bright as a button; dark as night; white as a sheet; big as a house; still as a statue . . .

No doubt many of these cliché similes owe as much to the attraction of alliteration as anything else. But children won't **know** that they are clichés unless someone tells them. See if you can add to the list, with the help of parents and anyone else you can involve, then use it as a resource.

 WRITING ACTIVITY: Rhyming clichés

Any extensive list is liable to contain a few rhymes, and this one is no exception. Get the children to see how many couplets they can find.

> As tough as old boots, As crazy as a coot
> As big as a house, As quiet as a mouse
> As sly as a fox, As strong as an ox
> As deaf as a post, As warm as toast
> As high as a kite, As dark as night
> As slimy as a snake, As thin as a rake
> As slow as a snail, As dead as a doornail
> As clear as a bell, Like a bat out of hell

Let them play around with different rhyming schemes:

> As tough as old boots
> As big as a house
> As crazy as a coot
> As quiet as a mouse   (ABAB)

As sly as a fox
As deaf as a post,
As warm as toast
As strong as an ox (ABBA)

As high as a kite
As slimy as a snake
As slow as a snail;
As dark as night
As thin as a rake
As dead as a doornail.
As clear as a bell,
Like a bat out of hell   (ABCABCDD)

There are umpteen variations, but what about the meaning? Well, anything can be given meaning, if you come up with the right title. How about *The Cliché Monster*?

 ## WRITING ACTIVITY: Creating new similes

Explain to the children that these cliché similes are all right for a bit of fun, but they have been used so much they're like a worn-out carpet in a posh hotel (or make up your own simile). The children in **your** class deserve better. They deserve Brand New Similes for their poems and stories.

With the whole class to begin with, use your cliché resource again to create some new versions, getting your inspiration from different 'subject' areas.

For example,

Animal: quiet as a caterpillar
Weather: quiet as a cloud
Feeling: quiet as a sulk
Facial: quiet as a frown
Clothes: quiet as grey socks
Place/time: quiet as the staff room at midnight
Object: quiet as a statue

Obviously, some clichés will lend themselves to this treatment more than others, and whether any of the results prove to be effective similes in practice would depend on the context into which they are placed. But, at least we're moving the children on by getting them to create something new.

WRITING ACTIVITY: Similes for smiles

For fun, or as the kick-off to a nonsense piece, the children could use the clichés to invent 'sarcastic' similes: quiet as a motorbike (noisy as a mouse); dark as a torch (bright as night); slow as a speedboat (fast as a snail).

Once you have generated 'similes' like these, you can start asking, Who? What? Why? Where? When? How? Which? to make them 'sensible' again:

> quiet as a motorbike without petrol; noisy as a mouse in tap shoes; dark as a torch with no battery; bright as night in the Arctic summer; slow as a speedboat in treacle; fast as a snail on a skateboard.

Any image generated in this way could be used as a kick-off for a poem or story, or saved up for possible insertion into a piece of creative writing.

WRITING ACTIVITY: More new similes

Those cliché similes that contain 'like' are harder for children to understand without explanation. Out of context, 'it's like flogging a dead horse' and doesn't tell you what this equine battering is being compared to.

While reminding the children that these phrases have been 'flogged to death' themselves, choose a few and give explanations.

> 'like flogging a dead horse' . . . doing something that is ineffective, a waste of time
> 'like a fish out of water' . . . when a person is, or feels, out of place
> 'like a dog with a bone' . . . could mean being chuffed or possessive or tenacious

Then get the children to liken these situations to new images.

> an ineffective action . . . it's like telling fire not to burn
> being out of place . . . he's like a duck in the desert
> being possessive . . . like a teacher with chocolate

Again, a simile that is created in this way could be used in a piece of creative writing, or the image can be taken literally and used as a poem/story kick-off.

In everyday speech, of course, we often drop the word 'like', as in 'I'm flogging a dead horse here'. And so, simile becomes metaphor.

Metaphor

Metaphors can make for more powerful writing than similes. With a metaphor, instead of comparing two things, we are stating that one thing **is** another. So the simile, 'His laugh was like thunder', could become the metaphor, 'His laugh was thunder', 'The thunder of his laugh', 'His laugh's thunder' or even 'His thunderous laugh', as in Ian Souter's poem, *The Great Water Giant* (p. 129). It's easy, therefore, to turn cliché similes into cliché metaphors:

'Simon was [like] a dog with a bone when it came to sharing.'

What isn't so easy for children is to come up with **original** metaphors. We can use the principle of 'Show don't tell' to create original metaphors. If I write, 'When David left the room, he was angry', I'm **telling** you that he was angry. But, if I write, 'When David left the room, he slammed the door behind him', I'm **showing** you how he was feeling, by showing his actions. And that's much more powerful writing. (See *A Poetry Teacher's Toolkit* Book 4, Ch. 1.)

Emotions are a good place to start. How else might David show his anger? By stamping his foot; by going red in the face; by breaking something; by banging his fist on the table; by shouting.

David was a fist
that crashed onto the table.
He was a stamping foot
and a shouting-red face.

David was a crystal vase
dashed onto the kitchen floor.

He was a slamming door.   M.J.

Similar treatment could be given to: happy, sad, lonely, angry, excited, jealous, frightened, greedy, lazy, hot, cold.

The Heron by Ted Hughes (p. 131)

I have included this poem not only for its metaphors, but also for its wonderful economy of words.

- 'The Sun's an iceberg [metaphor] / In the sky': probably not something that children will have observed, but this is one of those winter days when the sun is showing, but it's pale and gives no warmth. It even **looks** cold.
- 'In solid freeze / The fishes lie': in six words, Hughes shows us the fish, motionless under a covering of ice.
- 'Doomed is the Dab / Death leans above' (personification): without being told here, we know 'who' Death is, and why the fish is doomed. It was established in the title.

- 'But the Heron / Poised to stab': you need to have seen a heron fishing to appreciate this fully. It stands unmoving, with its neck coiled, until it feels certain of a catch. Then its neck uncoils and its stiletto beak jabs down to the fish.
- 'Has turned to iron [metaphor] / And cannot move': except, this heron has been careless. It has been so intent on fishing that it hasn't noticed the water freezing around its legs (something that also happens in *Tarka the Otter* if I remember rightly).
- The relationship of the words 'Doomed', 'Dab' and 'stab' says much about the poet's craft: 'Dab' is both alliterative with 'Doomed', and rhymes with 'stab'. You only get that kind of quality by working at your poem. My guess is that dab/stab came together first, and the alliterative 'Doomed' was chosen after.
- Although this is a rhyming poem, the rhyme is unobtrusive (particularly 'above'/'move') and doesn't conform to a pattern.

Creating more metaphors

- For a metaphor to be successful, the two elements must have at least one thing in common.
- But, to be original, they must be an unexpected combination.

Here's a way of achieving both aims . . . sometimes.

WRITING ACTIVITY: Creating new metaphors

Try this one yourself a few times before getting the kids to have a go. Without doing a full brainstorm (see *A Poetry Teacher's Toolkit* Book 3, Ch. 4), choose a topic and list a few associations. For example:

Moon: moonwalking; eclipse; tides; romance; crater; werewolf; madness.

The idea now is to get two of these elements to 'collide'. Try it with adjacent words to begin with.

His skill at moonwalking eclipsed his singing. (That's not bad, unless you're a fan of the former lead singer of The Jackson Five!)

After the eclipse, the tide of watchers ebbed away. (Cliché, yuk!)

Theirs was a tidal romance. (Not bad.)

So many romances she could remember began with walking on the moon, and ended up in a crater. (I like that one.)

The werewolf tore craters out of his victim. (Sorry about that one.)

She thought of love as a kind of madness; a werewolf that rampaged for a night or two, then thankfully disappeared, until the next full moon. (Mills and Boon eat your hearts out!)

Other pairings:

One silver bullet, and the werewolf was eclipsed.

When she left him, he slid into a crater of madness.

Metaphor versus Simile

There is a tendency to think of simile as a second-class metaphor. But, there's a bit more going on than that.

Rule of thumb: if you are planning more than one comparison, use simile:

My love is like a red, red rose
   That's newly sprung in June:
My love is like a melody
   That's sweetly played in tune.

'So fair art thou . . .'

The comparisons are made, the focus stays on 'My love', and the poet (Robert Burns) moves on.

If you're employing just one comparison, and you want to develop its theme, use metaphor.

My Love is a rose.
I gaze at her delicate beauty,
I drink the smell of her;
But she don't half scratch.   M.J.

The focus is transferred from 'My Love' to those qualities of a rose which she shares.

Grandpa by Berlie Doherty (p. 131)

In only four lines, using two similes and a metaphor, Berlie Doherty succeeds in painting an impressionistic portrait of a Grandpa whom we **feel** is loving and kindly, although we are not actually **told** so.

- 'Grandpa's hands are as rough as garden sacks': if that simile is as well chosen as I think it is, Grandpa is a gardener. What's more, he's got an old-fashioned potting-shed. (How do I know? Because **my** Grampy had one, that's how!)
- 'And as warm as pockets': still talking about his hands, but we **know** instinctively that Grandpa has a warm personality too. He's always happy to have his grand-daughter climb onto his lap. That's when she's studied his eyes.

- 'His skin is crushed paper round his eyes': the poet switches from simile to an effective metaphor for 'showing' Grandpa's wrinkles. But it gets better:
- 'Wrapping up their secrets': the metaphor is now extended. This is not just any paper – it's wrapping paper. Wrapping paper is bright and colourful, and is associated with happy surprises and celebration. Of course, some of the secrets (or memories) will not be pleasant ones, but this old feller has depth in his smiling eyes, and he continues to love life.

Is all that too fanciful? I don't think so . . . because, bringing my own memories and experience to the poem, that's what it says to me.

Personification

Personification means attributing human qualities to non-living objects or concepts. For example, the 'runaway' handkerchief in Charlotte Druitt Cole's *The Clothes-Line* (p. 130) was 'Flipping and flapping and flopping for fun'.

Giving human traits to an animal is covered by anthropomorphism, e.g. in *Indian Summer* by Emily Dickinson (p. 133), a few birds 'take a backward look'.

Other poems in this volume that demonstrate one, or both, of these devices are:

The Man in the Moon Stayed Up Too Late, by J. R. R. Tolkien (p. 35)
Extracts from *The Song of Hiawatha* by H. W. Longfellow (p. 39)
Cool Cat by Mike Jubb (p. 42)
Rockets by Mike Jubb (p. 78)
Weather is Full of the Nicest Sounds by Aileen Fisher (p. 102)
The Great Water Giant by Ian Souter (p. 129)
The Windmill by H. W. Longfellow (p. 132)
The Flint by Christina Rossetti (p. 134)

WRITING ACTIVITY: Practising personification

Get each child to choose something to personify: a piece of furniture; an aspect of weather; a natural feature; a toy; a machine; a building; a month or season. Then give them a verb to go with it; either the same verb for everyone, or distribute verbs randomly. Here are some ideas:

  takes, hopes, remembers, listens to, tells, feels like, brings, looks forward to, shows,
  looks for, reminds, teaches, dreams, dances, helps, guides.

So, they'll have something like: 'chair/remembers'. Now they have to make this into a sentence, e.g. 'The chair remembers when he was new.' Get the children to ask themselves questions about their sentence (Who? What? Why? Where? When? How? Which?). The ending on the verb can be changed.

The old armchair
in the ditch
could still remember
a time
when he made Amelia
comfortable.   M.J.

Putting it all together

I think of devices such as rhythm, rhyme, assonance, onomatopoeia, alliteration, simile, metaphor, and personification as components. Singly or in combinations, subtly or with a sledgehammer, they provide opportunities for endless diversity and invention.

The Great Water Giant by Ian Souter (p. 129)

Ian Souter skilfully blends a number of writing devices in *The Great Water Giant*. This well-crafted poem has rhythm (but not meter), rhyme ('gushes'/'slushes'), assonance ('thirsty earth'), onomatopoeia ('plishes' etc.), alliteration ('squelchy sky'), word shapes ('splooshes' etc.), metaphor (the whole poem is an extended metaphor: the rain **is** bath water), and personification (the Great Water Giant personifies, I suppose, the storm as distinct from the rain). These devices are used in subtle moderation to create a peach of a poem that works on the imagination, the ear and the eye; it's a poem that paints a picture of a jovial giant in the sky, letting out his bath water to give a rainy day that you feel you'd enjoy being out in.

The Great Water Giant will stand many repetitions, and is a gift for teacher performance if practised beforehand (see *A Poetry Teacher's Toolkit* Book 4, Ch. 4). Make your delivery of the words slow and deliberate. Squeeze the sound out of every syllable. Note which words demand particular emphasis, such as 'huge', 'roars', and '**thun**derous'. Milk the alliteration of 'spills out of a squelchy sky', the onomatopoeia of the rain words, and the final assonance of 'thirsty earth'.

I'm not saying that **every** poem must have **all** the sound tricks of the trade – I'm just pointing out how effective a combination can be.

THE LITERACY HOUR: YEARS 3 AND 4

National Literacy Strategy objectives: Years 3 and 4

Year 3
- To discuss choice of words and phrases that describe and create impact.
- To take account of the grammar and punctuation . . . when reading aloud.
- To infer the meaning of unknown words from context.

Year 4
- To understand the use of figurative language in poetry.
- To revise and extend work in Year 3 . . . and link to work on . . . figurative language in . . . poetry.
- To understand that vocabulary changes over time.

Chosen poem

The Clothes-Line by Charlotte Druitt Cole (p. 130)

Materials needed

Enlarged copies of the chosen poem (see 'Preparation'), one for the whole-class session and one for Group 1
Board or flipchart
Marker pens
A selection of pictures of inanimate objects
Pens, pencils, writing books/paper
Activity sheets (see 'Preparation')
Cassette recorder/player and blank cassette
Photocopiable sheet D (see 'Preparation')

Preparation

Enlarge the poem. Before the lesson, cover up all the text except for the title.

Make copies of the activity sheets for each child, according to achievement level (photocopiable sheets 4a, 4b, 4c on pp. 122–124).

Record the chosen poem onto the blank cassette, making sure you recite it at a speed that enables the children to switch the player on and off, without losing the meaning.

You could use only part of the poem, according to the achievement level of the group, if this is more appropriate.

Make copies of photocopiable sheet D (p. 128) for Group 5.

With the whole class

- Ask a volunteer to read the title and then invite the children to suggest what this poem might be about. Jot down on the board a few key words to refer to later. Does anyone have a clothes-line at home that is regularly used? What do many families use nowadays to dry the washing? Can the children suggest why? Tell the children you are going to read the poem and they should listen carefully to the way Charlotte Druitt Cole describes the washing.

- Share the poem, letting the children follow the text as you read. When you have finished, ask them whether they liked the poem and why or why not. Have a look at the key words jotted down at the beginning of the session – how accurate were the children's guesses?

- Can anyone tell you how the poet is describing the washing? When someone suggests that it is described as live creatures, focus on this and ask them how they know; can they give specific examples? ('Hand in hand they dance', 'Flutt'ring creatures', 'Like restive horses', 'fairy-tale witches', 'They shiver and skip', 'She flew like a bird', etc.)

- Explain that the poet has used several devices to put across this idea: similes – can anybody remember what a simile is? If not, remind the class ('Like restive horses', 'Like fairy-tale witches' and 'like a bird'); metaphors – again, ask what a metaphor is and if necessary, remind them ('Flutt'ring creatures', 'restive horses'); personification – can someone tell you what this is? ('Hand in hand they dance in a row', '. . . they caper and prance', 'They shiver and skip', '. . . or drowned in the sea'.)

- Do the children think these techniques are useful for putting across images in poetry? Why or why not? Do they think the description of the washing on the line is more vivid? Can they say why or why not? Are they able to imagine it more easily? Why or why not? What does the poet mean by the phrase 'Rounded in front, but hollow behind'? Have the children ever seen washing on the line that looks like this?

- What clues are there in the poem that it is not modern? ('Hither and thither', 'Flutt'ring', 'caper and prance', '. . . they wildly dance', '. . . the merry March wind', '. . . where she now can be'.) Are we likely to have a handkerchief in the washing nowadays? Why not?

- Tell the children they're going to do some more work on this in their groups.

Group and independent work (differentiated groups)

Group 1
Give out the enlarged copy of the poem and marker pens in three different colours. Ask the children to work together to find examples of similes, metaphors and personification in the poem. They should circle the examples they find, using the same colour for each type, for example, all similes in red, all metaphors in blue and all personification in green.

Group 2

Give out copies of activity sheets 4a (for lower achievers), 4b (for average achievers) and 4c (for higher achievers) and ask the children to complete them. Let them work in pairs for support if necessary.

Group 3

Put the pictures face down on the table and ask the group to work together. They should turn over the pictures one at a time and agree a simile, a metaphor and an example of personification for each picture. For example, a tree: 'The boy was tall, like a tree', (simile); 'The boy was a tall tree', (metaphor); 'The tree groaned painfully in the wind', (personification). They should write their examples in their books.

Group 4

Give the cassette player with the recorded cassette to the group. Ask them to make up an action play that can be performed to the poem, using the recorded version to help them rehearse. (This may need to be done away from the main classroom.)

Group 5

Give out copies of photocopiable sheet D for the children to complete (see activity above, p. 109). They could do this activity in pairs for support.

Plenary session (whole class)

- Use some of the inanimate pictures and brainstorm with the children a simile, a metaphor and personification for each one. Write them on the board or flipchart and invite the children to add more to them later.
- Does everyone understand what simile, metaphor and personification mean?
- As a class, recite the poem while the group which made up the action play gives a

THE LITERACY HOUR: YEARS 5 AND 6

National Literacy Strategy objectives: Years 5 and 6

Year 5
- To analyse . . . poetic style, use of forms and themes.
- To understand how writing can be adapted for different audiences.
- To investigate metaphorical expressions and figures of speech from everyday life.

Year 6
- To comment critically on the overall impact of a poem, showing how [the] language and theme have been developed.
- To adapt texts for particular . . . purposes.
- To understand how words and expressions have changed over time.

Chosen poem

The Windmill by H. W. Longfellow (p. 132)

Materials needed

Board or flipchart
Marker pens
Copy of the chosen poem (see 'Preparation')
Dictionaries
Copies of other poems featured in this chapter (see 'Preparation')
Pens, pencils, writing paper/books
Materials for making a collage
Activity sheets (see 'Preparation')
Noun and verb cards (see 'Preparation')

Preparation

Enlarge the chosen poem and cover it over.

Make copies of the activity sheets for each child, according to achievement level (photocopiable sheets 4aa, 4bb, 4cc on pp. 125–127).

Make copies of other poems listed at the beginning of the chapter, featured on pages 129–35 (you to determine quantity and choice), enough for each child in Group 3. Alternatively, make copies of other poems featuring personification.

Use either commercially produced noun cards or make your own with words such as 'chair', 'the sun', 'snow', 'house', 'summer', 'car', 'February', etc. Make cards with a verb written on each, such as 'wants', 'says', 'remembers', 'feels', etc. Make enough for Group 5 plus five more of each.

With the whole class

- Tell the children that you're going to read the first line of a poem and you want them to guess what it is about. Leaving the enlarged copy covered over, read 'Behold, a giant am I!' Ask for suggestions and list these on the board.
- Read a little more of the poem – do the children know yet what it is about?
- Uncover the poem and share the title, *The Windmill*. Was anyone right in their guess?
- Explain that the poem is by H. W. Longfellow (at this point, don't tell them when the poem was written). Spend a moment or two discussing what a windmill is and what it is used for (grinding corn or making electricity). Are there any windmills near school? What were/are they used for? Ask the children to pay attention to how Longfellow portrays the windmill in the poem.
- Share the poem with the children, allowing them to see the text as you read. Try, with expression and intonation, to put across the size and might of the windmill. When you have finished, ask the children what they thought of the poem. Encourage them to support their opinions with reasons and examples.
- Can anyone say what device Longfellow has used for the poem? If they don't know the word (personification) ask them to describe what he has done. What do they think of this technique? Does it add to the enjoyment of the poem? Why or why not? Ask the children to focus on the words and phrases that are examples of personification. Invite them to come up and use a coloured marker to highlight their suggestions. (By the time they have finished, almost the whole poem will be highlighted!)
- When do the children think the poem was written? (During the nineteenth century.) How do they know? List their examples of 'old-fashioned' language on the board. For example, 'Behold', '. . . the sound of flails' or '. . . threshing-floors'. What does the windmill mean by 'With my granite jaws I devour/The maize, and the wheat, and the rye'? What are 'flails' and 'threshing-floors'? How does the miller 'feed[s] me with his hands'? What happens when the windmill meets the wind 'face to face,/As a brave man meets his foe'? What is a foe? Are there any other words or phrases they don't understand? Together, work out the meanings, using the context and/or dictionaries.
- Ask the children how today's windmills (i.e. wind turbines) are different from the one in the poem?

Group and independent work (differentiated groups)

Group 1

Let the group agree a subject for a poem, using personification. For example, *The Car*, *The Wind*, *The House*, etc. Encourage them to brainstorm characteristics of their subject and jot down key words. Ask them to write a short poem, personifying the subject. Remind them it doesn't have to rhyme. They could work either individually, in pairs or as a group, either with or without your support, according to achievement level.

Group 2

Give out copies of activity sheets 4aa (for lower achievers), 4bb (for average achievers) and 4cc (for higher achievers) and ask the children to complete them.

Group 3

Give out the copies of the other featured poems listed at the beginning of the chapter. Ask the children to work together to decide how they are examples of personification. They should either highlight the examples with coloured marker pens or write them down.

Group 4

Ask the group to make a collage of the windmill. They should select a few lines from the poem to illustrate their picture and write them at the bottom.

Group 5

Put the noun and verb cards on the table, face down. Let the children play a game where they turn over one card from each pile and then make up a sentence personifying the noun, using the verb (see activity above, p. 114). For example, if they turned over 'a tree' and 'listens', their sentence could read *The tree listens to the noise of the traffic*.

Plenary session (whole class)

- Make sure everyone understands what 'personification' means. Ask a volunteer to explain it to the class.
- Share the poem once more, encouraging the children to join in. They should use voice, expression and intonation to put across the characteristics of the windmill in the poem.

SHEET 4a

Name _____

Write 'simile', 'metaphor' or 'personification' beside each of these examples:

The cat was a fierce lion _____

The flowers danced in the wind _____

My mum is thin like a stick _____

The football flew into the goal _____

Dad ran as fast as a cheetah _____

The moon was a silver penny _____

Now complete these similes and metaphors:

Mum's cake was as tasty as _____

The greedy boy is a _____

The tall tree is a _____

The baby was tiny like a _____

Make up a simile and a metaphor of your own:

_____

_____

SHEET 4b

Name _____

Write 'simile', 'metaphor' or 'personification' beside each of these examples:

Dad's car was a rocket _____

My teddy is cuddly like a rabbit _____

Ice touches with freezing fingers _____

The sun is a golden ball _____

Roses are as red as blood _____

The candles smiled out their light _____

The trees were asleep all winter _____

My bed is a slab of stone _____

The house windows glinted like diamonds _____

Now complete these similes and metaphors:

The butter was as soft as _____

Our teacher's desk is a _____

Grandad's snoring was a _____

The bad egg stank like _____

The puppies wriggled like _____

The storm was a _____

Make up a simile and a metaphor of your own:

_____

_____

© Collette Drifte and Mike Jubb (2002) *A Poetry Teacher's Toolkit*, Book 2. London: David Fulton Publishers.

SHEET 4c

Name _____

Write 'simile', 'metaphor' or 'personification' beside each of these examples:

My bike is a racehorse _____

The wind shouted through the trees _____

Aunty Beryl is as funny as a clown _____

Chocolate is edible gold _____

Mum's old coat snuggles around her _____

Dad's snoring is as loud as thunder _____

The moon was a silver penny _____

My mum is thin like a skeleton _____

The football flew into the goal _____

Now complete these similes and metaphors:

Mum's bike is as old as _____

The nasty boy is a _____

The angry shark was a _____

Toadstools are poisonous like _____

The fat dog was a _____

Dad's really funny, like a _____

The leaking pipe was a _____

Her baby's ears are like _____

Make up a simile and a metaphor of your own:

_____

_____

SHEET 4aa

Name _____

Read *The Windmill* by H. W. Longfellow.

Which of these verbs are in the poem? Circle them with a coloured pen:

I see   I sing   I shout   I stand   I play

Write three more verbs from the poem:

_____   _____   _____

Choose one of these and draw a circle around it:

a table   a flower   the wind   a car

Now choose one of these and draw a circle around it:

feels   hears   remembers   wants

Put them together and finish the sentence. Here's an example:

A flower feels happy in the sun.

_____

SHEET 4bb

Name _____

Read *The Windmill* by H. W. Longfellow.

Which of these verbs are in the poem? Circle them with a coloured pen:

I sing   I shout   I stand   I jump   I hear   I play   I see

Write four more verbs from the poem:

_____   _____   _____   _____

Choose two of these and draw circles around them:

a chair   a tree   a football   the sun   a bike

Now choose two of these and draw circles around them:

dreams   wants   hears   remembers   thinks

Put them together and finish the sentences. Here's an example:

A flower feels happy in the sun.

_____

_____

SHEET 4cc

Name _____

Read *The Windmill* by H. W. Longfellow.

Which of these verbs are in the poem? Circle them with a coloured pen:

I devour   I shout   I stand   I play   I eat   I dance   I see

Write five more verbs from the poem:

_____   _____   _____   _____   _____

Choose three of these and draw circles around them:

a cooker   an apple   a football   the moon   a candle

Now choose three of these and draw circles around them:

teaches   dreams   wishes   listens   reminds

Put them together and finish the sentences. Here's an example:

A flower feels happy in the sun.

_____

_____

PHOTOCOPIABLE SHEET D

Name _____

Make some similes for the words below. For example,

Quiet: Animal: quiet as a caterpillar   Weather: quiet as a cloud

Feeling: quiet as a sulk   Facial: quiet as a frown

Clothes: quiet as grey socks   Place/time: quiet as the staff room

Object: quiet as a statue   at midnight

Noisy: Animal: noisy as _____   Weather: noisy as _____

Feeling: noisy as _____   Facial: noisy as _____

Clothes: noisy as _____   Place/time: noisy as _____

Object: noisy as _____

Large: Animal: _____   Weather: _____

Feeling: _____   Facial: _____

Clothes: _____   Place/time: _____

Object: _____

Scared: Animal: _____   Weather: _____

Feeling: _____   Facial: _____

Clothes: _____   Place/time: _____

Object: _____

The Great Water Giant

Ian Souter

The Great Water Giant
has finished his bath.

He pulls the huge plug
out of the clouds.
He roars his thunderous laugh
and a wet, slippery waterfall
spills out of a squelchy sky.

'Look out below,' he seems to shout,
as the water

```
s       p       g
p       l       u
l   s   i   p   s   s
o   p   s   l   h   l
o   l   h   o   e   u
s   a   e   s   s   s
h   s   s   h       h
e   h       e       e
s   e       s       s
    s
```

and soaks deep into the thirsty earth.

The Clothes-Line

Charlotte Druitt Cole

Hand in hand they dance in a row,
Hither and thither, and to and fro,
Flip! Flap! Flop! and away they go –
Flutt'ring creatures as white as snow.
Like restive horses they caper and prance;
Like fairy-tale witches they wildly dance;
Rounded in front, but hollow behind,
They shiver and skip in the merry March wind.
One I saw dancing excitedly,
Struggling so wildly till she was free,
Then, leaving pegs and clothes-line behind her,
She flew like a bird, and no one can find her.
I saw her gleam, like a sail, in the sun,
Flipping and flapping and flopping for fun.
Nobody knows where she now can be,
Hid in a ditch, or drowned in the sea.
She was my handkerchief not long ago,
But she'll never come back to my pocket, I know.

Grandpa

Berlie Doherty

Grandpa's hands are as rough as garden sacks
And as warm as pockets.
His skin is crushed paper round his eyes,
Wrapping up their secrets.

The Heron

Ted Hughes

The Sun's an iceberg
In the sky.
In solid freeze
The fishes lie.

Doomed is the Dab.
Death leans above –

But the Heron
Poised to stab
Has turned to iron
And cannot move.

The Windmill

H. W. Longfellow

Behold, a giant am I!
Aloft here in my tower,
With my granite jaws I devour
The maize, and the wheat, and the rye,
And grind them into flour.

I look down over the farms;
In the fields of grain I see
The harvest that is to be,
And I fling to the air my arms,
For I know it is all for me.

I hear the sound of the flails
Far off, from the threshing-floors
In barns, with their open doors,
And the wind, the wind in my sails,
Louder and louder roars.

I stand here in my place,
With my foot on the rock below,
And whichever way it may blow
I meet it face to face,
As a brave man meets his foe.

And while we wrestle and strive,
My master, the miller, stands
And feeds me with his hands;
For he knows who makes him thrive,
Who makes him lord of lands.

The Windmill **(continued)**

On Sundays I take my rest;
Church-going bells begin
Their low, melodious din;
I cross my arms on my breast,
And all is peace within.

Extract from *Indian Summer*

Emily Dickinson

These are the days when Birds come back –
A very few – a Bird or two –
To take a backward look.

These are the days when skies resume
The old – old sophistries of June –
A blue and gold mistake.

Oh fraud that cannot cheat the Bee –
Almost thy plausibility
Induces my belief.

Till ranks of seeds their witness bear –
And softly thro' the altered air
Hurries a timid leaf.

The Flint

Christina Rossetti

An emerald is as green as grass,
A ruby red as blood,
A sapphire shines as blue as heaven;
But a flint lies in the mud.
A diamond is a brilliant stone
To catch the world's desire;
An opal holds a rainbow light,
But a flint holds fire.

Boats Sail on the Rivers

Christina Rossetti

Boats sail on the rivers,
    And ships sail on the seas;
But clouds that sail across the sky
    Are prettier far than these.

There are bridges on the rivers,
    As pretty as you please;
But the bow that bridges heaven,
    And overtops the trees,
And builds a bridge from earth to sky,
    Is prettier far than these.

If I Knew

Anon.

If I knew the box where the smiles were kept,
    No matter how large the key
Or strong the bolt, I would try so hard,
    'Twould open, I know, for me;
Then over the land and sea broadcast
    I'd scatter the smiles to play,
That the children's faces might hold them fast
    For many and many a day.

If I knew a box that was large enough
    To hold all the frowns I meet,
I would gather them, every one,
    From nursery, school, and street;
Then, folding and holding, I'd pack them in,
    And turn the monster key,
And hire a giant to drop the box
    To the depths of the deep, deep sea.

Further Reading

This is not meant to be a definitive list of poetry books for children, just a few that we particularly like (apologies for all the great collections that we've left out).

Reference

Roget's Thesaurus
The Penguin Rhyming Dictionary
The Oxford Spelling Dictionary

Collections by individual poets

Gerard Benson, *The Magnificent Callisto* (Blackie 1992)
Charles Causley, *Collected Poems for Children* (Macmillan UK 1996)
Eleanor Farjeon, *Blackbird Has Spoken* (Macmillan UK 1999)
John Foster, *Word Wizard* (Oxford University Press 2001)
Lindsay MacRae, *How to Avoid Kissing Your Parents in Public* (Puffin 2000)
Colin McNaughton, *There's an Awful Lot of Weirdos in our Neighbourhood* (Walker Books 2000)
Gareth Owen, *Collected Poems for Children* (Macmillan UK 2000)
Brian Patten, *Juggling with Gerbils* (Puffin 2000)
Robert Louis Stevenson, *A Child's Garden of Verses* (various editions available)
J. R. R. Tolkien, *The Adventures of Tom Bombadil* (George Allen and Unwin 1961)

Anthologies

John Agard and Grace Nichols (eds) *A Caribbean Dozen* (Walker Books 1994)
John Agard, Wendy Cope, Roger McGough, Adrian Mitchell, Brian Patten and Colin McNaughton, *Another Day on Your Foot and I Would Have Died* (Macmillan Children's Books 1996)
Jill Bennett and Mary Rees, *Spooky Poems* (Heinemann 1989)
Jill Bennett and Nick Sharratt, *Playtime Poems* (Oxford University Press 1995)
John Foster, *A First Poetry Book* (Oxford University Press 1979)
John Foster, *Another First Poetry Book* (Oxford University Press 1987)
John Foster, *Another Second Poetry Book* (Oxford University Press 1988)
John Foster, *Let's Celebrate Festival Poems* (Oxford University Press 1989)

John Foster, *A Blue Poetry Paintbox* (Oxford University Press 1994)

John Foster, *A Green Poetry Paintbox* (Oxford University Press 1994)

John Foster, *Action Rhymes* (Oxford University Press 1996)

John Foster, *Crack Another Yolk and other wordplay poems* (Oxford University Press 1996)

John Foster, *First Verses* (Oxford University Press 1996)

John Foster, *Food Rhymes* (Oxford University Press 1998)

John Foster, *More First Verses* (Oxford University Press 1998)

Sophie Hannah, *The Box Room* (Orchard Books 2001) (recommended pantoum called *The Swimming Pool*)

Brian Moses, *Performance Poems* (Southgate 1996)

Brian Patten (ed.) *The Puffin Book of Utterly Brilliant Poetry* (Puffin Books 2001)

Michael Rosen, *A Spider Bought a Bicycle and other poems for young children* (Kingfisher Books 1992)

Will Self, *Junk Mail* (Penguin 1996)

Kaye Umansky, *Nonsense Counting Rhymes* (Oxford University Press 1999)

Shape poetry

Paul Cookson, *The Works* (Macmillan 2001)

Gina Douthwaite, *Picture a Poem* (Hutchinson 1994)

Gina Douthwaite, *What Shapes an Ape* (Hutchinson 2001)

John Foster, *Crack Another Yolk* (Oxford University Press 1996)

Magazine

Literacy and Learning, published by the Questions Publishing Company Ltd

Glossary

Acrostic
A poetic form which is organised by the initial letters of a key word, either at the beginning of lines, or with lines arranged around them.

Whistling wildly   Blowing
In a   rain
Northern   round
Direction   a**n**d round

Adagio
A slow tempo.

Alliteration
A phrase in which adjacent or closely connected words begin with the same phoneme: one wet Wellington; free phone; several silent, slithering snakes.

Alphabets
Poems based on alphabetical order.

Ambigram
This is one name given to words that can be read in more than one way, or from more than one vantage point, either as themselves such as 'NOON' and 'suns' (upside down), or as a different word ('PAT'/'TAP'). Obviously, this ties in well with symmetry, and upper case gives different results from lower.

Anagram
A word or phrase formed by rearranging the letters of another word or phrase.

Analysis
An examination of the elements within a poem.

Anthology
A published collection of poems by several or many poets.

Anthropomorphism
Attributing human qualities to animals. See also **Personification**.

Antonym
A word with a meaning opposite to another: hot/cold, light/dark, light/heavy.
A word may have more than one word as an antonym: cold – hot/warm; big – small/tiny/little/titchy. See **Thesaurus**.

Appreciation
Added enjoyment of poetry through some knowledge of its elements. See **Analysis**.

Archaic language
No longer in ordinary use, though possibly retained for special purposes. The National Literacy Strategy requires that children learn 'to identify clues which suggest poems are older'.

Assonance
The rhyming of vowel sounds (but not consonants) in nearby words: such as in 'time' and 'light'. There is some overlap with near-rhymes here, because assonance is also the use of identical consonants with different vowels: such as in chilled/called/fold/mild/failed/hurled.

Beat
Main accent or rhythmic unit in music or verse.

Brainstorming
A joint discussion about a particular subject in order to pool knowledge, and to generate new ideas.

Caesura
A pause in a line of poetry (either at the end of the line, or mid-line), indicated by punctuation, a line break, or the natural flow of the language.

Calligram
A poem, or graphic, in which the calligraphy, the formation of the letters or the font selected, represents an aspect of the poem's subject: a poem about fear might be written in shaky letters to represent trembling; the word BRICKS could be printed in a brick-type font. See **Concrete poem** and **Shape poetry**.

Cinquain
A poem with a standard syllable pattern: 5 lines and a total of 22 syllables in the sequence: 2–4–6–8–2.

Cliché
An overused phrase or opinion: over the moon; flogging a dead horse; as sure as eggs is eggs.

Compound words
A word made up of two or more other words. There are three forms of compound word:
    closed form: football, headrest, broomstick
    hyphenated form: son-in-law, over-the-counter, six-year-old
    open form: post office, frying pan, full moon

Concrete poem
A poem in which the layout of the words represents some aspect of the subject. In some cases, these poems are presented as sculptures. Concrete poems blur the distinction between visual and linguistic art. See also **Calligram** and **Shape poetry**.

Crescendo
A passage gradually increasing in loudness or intensity; progress towards a climax.

Dactyl
A metrical foot consisting of one long (or stressed) syllable followed by two short (or unstressed) syllables (˘ ¯ ¯): **butt**erfly, **round**about, **bick**ering.

Diminuendo
A passage gradually decreasing in loudness or intensity.

Drafting/redrafting
The writing of initial and subsequent versions of a text, incorporating changes or revisions before the final version.

Dynamics
In poetry, as in music, a good performance requires variations in pace, pitch and volume. See also **Adagio**; **Caesura**; **Crescendo**; **Diminuendo**; **Pitch**; **Presto**; **Tempo**; **Timbre**.

Emphasis
A stress on a particular letter, phoneme, syllable or word.

Enjambment
In poetry, the continuation of a sentence without pause beyond the end of a line.

Exact rhyme
See **Rhyme**.

Expression
Using intonation to convey the meaning of a text. See also **Performance**.

Found verse
A piece of prose, from a source such as a newspaper, which is edited and presented as a poem.

Free verse
Poetry which is not constrained by patterns of rhyme or rhythm.

Full rhyme
See **Rhyme**.

Gunsaku
A group of haiku or tanka on a single subject which illuminates the subject from various

points of view, but can be read independently; e.g. a group of children could tackle the subject of 'Winter' by sharing out combinations of the following aspects: weather, animal hibernation, migration, difficulties for birds and animals, deciduous trees, conifers, a festival, colour, day length, etc.

Haiku

A Japanese form of poetry, widely thought in the West to be three lines of 5–7–5 syllables respectively. In truth, the form is much more flexible than that. It has always evolved, and is still evolving.

Half-rhymes

Multi-syllabic words in which the final syllable rhymes, e.g. camping/jumping. One of the examples of a half-rhyme given in the glossary of the National Literacy Strategy is 'polish/relish'. The other example given ('pun/man') is, in fact, classed as *near-rhyme*. See also **Rhyme**.

Hidden words

A type of wordplay in which one word is 'hidden' in the conjunction of two others. For example,

where do you hide a house?
round people w*ho use*d to live in a field

Homophones

Words that sound the same but have different meanings, and often different spellings.

Iamb (or Iambus)/Iambic

A metrical foot consisting of one short (or unstressed) syllable followed by one long (or stressed) syllable (‾ ˘): I **wan**dered **lone**ly **as** a **cloud** that **floats** on **high** o'er **vales** and **hills.**

INSET

In-service education and training. Further training or professional development for teachers or other educational practitioners.

Internal rhyme

The placement of rhyming words within a line of poetry, rather than at the end. The National Literacy Strategy example is:

'**Th**ough the threat of s**n**ow was gr**ow**ing sl**ow**ly'; in fact, 'gr**ow**ing sl**ow**ly' is *assonance*.

Intonation

The modulation of the voice during speech or reading.

Kenning

A compound expression used in Old English and Norse poetry, which names something without using its name, e.g. *mouse catcher = cat*. A kenning is, therefore, not a poem in itself, but a poem can be a list of kennings about one subject.

Kick-offs

Within this series, a *kick-off* is a strategy that will get children writing immediately, without 'thinking' too much.

Layout

The physical arrangement of words on the page.

Limerick

A five-line verse, usually comic, with the rhyme scheme AABBA, and the following stress pattern.

A **dark**-haired young **Princ**ess was **fond**
Of **kiss**ing a **frog** in the **pond**.
But it **made** the frog **wince**
Cos he **was**n't a **prince**,
And be**sides** that, he **want**ed a **blonde**.
[M.J.]

Line break

The point at which a poet chooses to end a line. This is particularly relevant to non-metric poetry in which line breaks are used as a form of punctuation.

Metaphor

Where the writer writes about something as if it were really something else. A metaphor can take several forms: his voice was thunder; his thunderous voice; his voice of thunder; the thunder of his voice. See also **Personification** and **Simile**.

Meter

Lines of poetry with a specified number of measures (or feet), e.g. a pentameter has five measures. There are various types of metrical foot. See **Dactyl**, **Iamb**, and **Trochee**.

Monosyllabic
Words or sounds consisting of only one syllable (and they have to invent a five-syllable word to describe it!).

Narrative poem
A poem that tells a story.

National Literacy Strategy
The official literacy curriculum taught in state schools in England and Wales.

Near-rhymes
Ones that you can get away with if you're not a slave to exact rhyme, e.g. can/men; stricken/picking. It's subjective; what the poet is happy with, because meaning is more important. See **Half-rhymes** and **Rhyme**.

Nonsense poems
A poem 'not of this world', but which makes perfect sense within its own parameters. There is a grey area between 'nonsense' and 'fantasy'.

Objectives
The educational targets or goals of the National Literacy Strategy.

Onji
Japanese sound units similar to, but different from, syllables.

Onomatopoeia
Words that echo sounds associated with their meaning: clang, hiss, crash, cuckoo.

Palindrome
A word or phrase that is the same when read left–right or right–left: kayak; Hannah; was it a cat I saw. Palindromes also exist where the word order is reversed, e.g. You and Mary only saw sweet Sally Little, and little Sally Sweet saw only Mary and you.

Pantoum/Pantun
A form of poetry originating in Malaysia in which the second line of each verse becomes

the first line of the following verse, sometimes with a slight variation. There may also be a link between the final and the first verses making the poem 'circular'.

Patterns
Regular formats found within poetry. They can be patterns of rhyme, rhythm, verse or line, for example.

Pentameter
A line of poetry consisting of five metrical feet.

Performance
The reciting of a poem using expression, intonation, pitch, volume, facial gestures and actions to convey the meaning, i.e. not simply reading the text.

Personification
A form of *metaphor* in which language relating to human action, motivation and emotion is used to refer to non-human agents or objects or abstract concepts, e.g. The chair obviously resented this demand on its strength; His jealousy took charge of him.

Pitch
The degrees of highness or lowness of the tone of voice during speech.

Polysyllabic
Words or sounds of more than one syllable.

Portmanteau words
New words that are blended from two or more existing words: brunch = breakfast + lunch; to crawble = to crawl under the table.

Prefix
A morpheme that can be added to the beginning of a word to change its meaning: in/edible, un/controllable, dis/agreeable.

Presto
Quick tempo.

Prose
Written language which does not follow poetic or dramatic forms.

Pun
A play on words, e.g. the maths teacher had divided loyalties; use of words with similar sounds, but different meaning, to 'humorous' effect, e.g. 'I can't bare it,' said Teddy.

Quatrain
A verse of four lines, usually with alternate rhymes.

Recite
To repeat aloud a poem from memory, particularly as a *performance*.

Redrafting
See **Drafting/redrafting**.

Redundancies
Words or phrases that can be removed from a text without affecting its essential meaning.

Reflected alliteration
Collette Drifte's term for alliteration that is transposed or 'reflected', e.g. . . . *chance of shade / cushion in the chair* (from *Home* by Rupert Brooke).

Rensaku
A longer work composed of individual haiku or tanka which function as stanzas of the whole, and are not independent.

Rhyme, Exact rhyme and Full rhyme
Words containing the same rime in their final syllable, or syllables, are said to rhyme. Single-syllable rhymes, e.g. moon / spoon, are referred to as male rhymes; where more than one syllable rhymes, e.g. dressing / messing, these are said to be female rhymes. See **Half-rhymes** and **Near-rhymes**.

Rhyming couplet
Two successive lines which rhyme at the ends.

Rhyming dictionary
A book of wordlists arranged according to rhyme. There's more than one on the market, but *The Penguin Rhyming Dictionary* (ISBN 0-14-051136-9) is very user friendly and is highly recommended.

Rhyming slang
An idiomatic form of speech where the spoken phrase rhymes with its (usually unspoken) meaning. For example, 'apples and pears' meaning 'stairs'. The two best known forms of rhyming slang are Cockney and Australian.

Rhythm
A pattern formed by a measured flow of words determined by long and short and / or accented and unaccented syllables.

Shape poetry
A generic term, covering both *calligrams* and *concrete poems*; a poem in which layout of the words reflects an aspect of the subject.

Show don't tell
A writer's 'trick of the trade'. It is generally stronger writing to say, for example, 'He banged his fist on the table' (showing the emotion) than 'He was angry' (merely telling).

Simile
A figure of speech involving the comparison of one thing with another thing of a different kind, as an illustration or ornament. Similes usually, but not necessarily, contain the word 'like' or 'as': 'He felt like a duck in the desert'; 'As quiet as a cloud'. See also **Metaphor** and **Personification**.

Spoonerism
Transposition of the initial letters of two words, giving an alternate phrase. For example, 'a darling snog'.

Stanza
A 'verse' or set of lines in poetry, the pattern of which is often repeated throughout the poem. However, stanzas can be of different lengths within the same poem.

Stress
An accent or emphasis on a word or syllable.

Structure
The format or layout of a text.

Suffix
A morpheme that is added to the end of a word. For example, 'scope' in 'telescope' and 'microscope'.

Syllable
A phonetic unit usually consisting of one vowel sound with a consonant before and after.

Synonyms
Words that have the same, or very similar, meaning: little/small. English is so rich in synonyms that overuse of any word is easily avoided. See **Thesaurus**.

Tanka
Meaning 'short poem'. A Japanese poem that has a **typical** form of 5–7–5–7–7 *syllables* (Japanese *onji*). Tanka has a history of about 13 centuries, as opposed to about three centuries for *haiku*, so is **not** based on the haiku as stated in the National Literacy Strategy document.

Tautology
Use of an extra word in a phrase or sentence which unnecessarily repeats an idea: the **annual** event is staged **yearly**; a **sudden surge** of water ('sudden' being part of the meaning of 'surge'). See also **Redundancies**.

Template
A solid outline representing an object or shape, used to draw around.

Tempo
The speed at which a piece of poetry is *recited*. The tempo can be varied within a poem to give a more interesting *performance*.

Tetrameter
A line of poetry consisting of four metrical feet.

Thesaurus
A reference text which groups words and phrases by meaning and association.

Timbre
The distinctive character or tone of a voice used while *reciting*.

Tongue-twisters
A sequence of words which is difficult to pronounce correctly and/or quickly.

Trochee/trochaic
In poetry, a metrical foot consisting of a long followed by a short syllable, or an accented followed by an unaccented syllable, e.g. **Ne**ver **on** a **Sun**day, **dar**ling.

Word morphing
A phrase coined to describe the transformation of one word into another by changing one letter, e.g. CAT → CAN. This can be expanded into strings, with three-letter words being easiest: CAT → CAN → MAN → MEN; FACE → FACT → PACT → PART → PORT; TWITS → TWINS → TWINE → SWINE → SHINE → SHONE.

Wordplay
A generic term which includes: *puns, word morphing, anagrams, calligrams, palindromes, hidden words*.

Index